The Naked Eye Potted Thesis Series

Our Potted Thesis Series consists of concise, layperson-friendly versions of doctoral and other research theses. The aim is to make accessible the ideas and wisdom of people whose academic *oeuvre* may otherwise languish in eternal obscurity in a university library. Our 'potted' versions intend to engage the reader in the excitement that first brought the researcher to their topic, and so may be more polemical than the original. While the requirements of academic rigour can weigh down a thesis with indigestible chapters on methodology and statistics, the Potted Thesis version brings to the fore the kernel of the idea and the meat of the discussion. For those who are interested, the detail of the research and the references that supported it are available in the original thesis publication.

Dr David Pendleton's book *Kick-off* started life as a PhD thesis submitted to De Montfort University, England. The title of the thesis was *Sport and the Victorian City: The development of commercialised spectator sport, Bradford 1836-1908*. The full thesis can be accessed through our website here:
http://nakedeyepublishing.co.uk/sport-and-the-victorian-city/

If you have a thesis that you think might benefit from a similar treatment, please read the further information on our website and write to us.

www.nakedeyepublishing.co.uk

The Author

David Pendleton is one of the north's leading historians of sport and leisure. He is currently the editor of the Bradford Antiquary, the journal of the Bradford Historical and Antiquarian Society which has been in publication since 1881. David appeared on national and regional TV and radio during his four years as editor of the Bradford City AFC supporters' fanzine 'The City Gent'. He has written for local and national newspapers including The Guardian, Sport First, Bradford Telegraph & Argus and The Yorkshire Post. From its inception in 2005 to its closure in 2012 (due to the construction of a free school) David was the curator of the Bantamspast Museum, the museum of Bradford City AFC at Valley Parade.

Also by David Pendleton

Along the Midland Road (with J. Dewhirst) Bradford City Association Football Club, Bradford, 1997

Glorious 1911, and the golden age of Bradford City 1908-15 bantamspast, Shipley, 2010

Paraders, the one hundred and twenty five year history of Valley Parade bantamspast, Shipley, 2011

'Culture, Tourism and Residential Development: the regeneration of Bradford's Little Germany warehouse district' in *A Collection of Essays on Place, Skills and Governance in the Yorkshire and Humber Region* Leeds Metropolitan University, Leeds, 2010

'Holidaymaking on the Edge: erosion, marginality and preservation, at Skipsea, Yorkshire', UK in *The International Journal of Tourism History*, Vol. 4, No. 3, September 2012

Kick-off

The start of spectator sports

Naked Eye Publishing

© David Pendleton 2018

All rights reserved

Book design and typesetting by Naked Eye

ISBN: 9781910981061

www.nakedeyepublishing.co.uk

Acknowledgements

I would like to acknowledge the staff of De Montfort University, in particular my PhD supervisors Professor Tony Collins and Neil Carter.

I would also like to thank the staff of Bradford Local Studies Library, Bradford Industrial Museum and the West Yorkshire Archive Service for their help and interest. The generosity and assistance given to me by officials and supporters of Bradford and Bingley RUFC, Bradford Bulls RLFC, Bradford Cricket League, Bradford City AFC and Bradford Park Avenue AFC have been invaluable. Many other individuals, including Chris Ambler, John Ashton, Mick Callaghan, John Dewhirst, Brian Heywood, Mick Pendleton, Dave Russell and John K. Walton played a role in bringing this work to its conclusion.

For proofreading and editorial comments, I and my publisher are grateful to Jeannie Williams; also to Phil Hopwood, Alison Marshall, Dave Scally and Mike Vickerman for additional comments.

This book is dedicated to the memory of my late father, Ernest Pendleton, who pushed me through the turnstiles at Park Avenue and Valley Parade at a tender age. Thus began an obsession that remains with me to this day.

Contents

Editor's Foreword 1

The revolution that sparked a revolution 5

Publicans - the entertainment entrepreneurs 13

Workers and women: cricket's segregations 21

The rise of rugby 35

Profits and players: sport as a business 49

The coming of the rugby and football leagues 63

The rise and decline of rugby's Northern Union 73

A match made in heaven: trams and cricket 85

The City of Bradford and Bradford City – a double birth 91

Football comes to Valley Parade 103

Sport at war: rugby vs football 107

'Ruinous departures': the triumph of tribalism 115

The Curious Case of Bradford (Park Avenue) AFC and the Southern Football League 123

A common goal 129

Recommended books 132

Editor's Foreword

This is the story of the start of sport as we know it today: how our most established international spectator sports, namely football, rugby and cricket, owe their origins to the working masses in the burgeoning Victorian cities of Great Britain.

Herein lies an epic tale against the backdrop of revolutionary times, an epoque of mass migration from small tight-knit rural communities into faceless and challenging 'satanic' urban centres during the onward march of Britain's world-leading Industrial Revolution. Massive social regrouping took place, with men and women instinctively joining together in new ways to regain the security of the belonging and sharing that people had grown up with in former times. Vital new community bonds evolved, whether through church and chapel or through social and sporting activities. This book shows how, for the grafters in the new industries, spectator sport became essential to the survival and wellbeing of the masses during decades of tumultuous social change.

For the full story of how sport enjoyed by British working men and women in the nineteenth century became the international social phenomenon it is today, we need look no further than one Victorian boom-town among northern England's rugged hills. That place is Bradford.

While Manchester, Leeds, Sheffield, Burnley and the rest get mentions, Bradford illustrates Britain's sporting revolution better than any other city, in tandem with its sensational rise to become the wool capital of the world. Bradford's pre-1914 sporting landscape was phenomenal. How come Bradford had not one but two professional football teams, a professional rugby league team and a semi-professional cricket league? Although the sporting prowess of cities such as Manchester and Sheffield have come to dwarf Bradford's sporting scene, Bradford's role in the development of today's global spectator sports remails uniquely significant.

Of women's early interest in sport we will learn sadly little. It goes without saying that Victorian Britain was deeply patriarchal, despite its presiding queen. A dearth of historical records regarding women's involvement in sport offers an impression that nineteenth century sporting life was an almost exclusively male domain. Was the doughty Emma Sharp (chapter 2) practically the only 'sportswoman', if her activity can be so termed, in nineteenth century Bradford's history?

Dave Pendleton's unfolding story details women's effective debarment from participation in spectator sports. Women may anyway have been largely uninterested and disengaged. The proportion of women among spectators has gone (largely) unrecorded, as has whether any women were among the publicans taking the bets at the early contests. Early photographs of sporting events would certainly tend to show a great sea of (men's) flat caps, barely punctuated by any persons differently attired.

Whatever the make-up of those early audiences, Dave Pendleton's account will fascinate all readers of whatever gender. His tale begins with a joyful crowd on the city's streets one spring evening in 1911. One would like to think that women as well as men were part of this proud, ecstatic celebration…

Sue Vickerman

Kick-off

1
The revolution that sparked a revolution

On the evening of the 26th of April 1911, Bradford City's team arrived at Bradford Exchange railway station after winning the Football Association Cup following a one-nil victory over Newcastle United in a replayed final at Old Trafford. One hundred thousand people, roughly a third of the entire population of the city, lined the streets to welcome home the victorious team. The Lord Mayor boarded the train to give the team a civic welcome.

Fifty years earlier, codified football (football played according to rules formally laid out by an organisation) did not even exist in Bradford. However, by 1911 a professional football team comprising eight Scotsmen, two Englishmen and one Irishman was being embraced as an integral part of the city's identity and progression from market town to one of the world's leading industrial cities. Even the new FA Cup trophy was a manifestation of Bradford's booming economy: it had been designed in the city by the jewellers Fattorini's.

The celebrations which seemingly united Bradford hid the fact that the city had a contested identity in sport. Bradford (Park Avenue) Association Football Club had been formed in 1907, while Bradford Northern was the city's representative in the rugby league. But despite this disunity, Bradford's sporting culture, largely based around professional team sport, was vibrant.

The development of that sporting culture from the informal and raucous to the regularised and professional, in tandem with the development of the physical city itself, makes 'sport' a metaphor for the city of Bradford's prowess and progress. Of all British cities, Bradford's history offers a prime demonstration of the origins of today's international spectator sports.

Britain's Industrial Revolution was the precursor of the revolution in sport. So what was it about the rise of industry in the early Victorian era that facilitated Bradford's first sporting leisure activities? The population explosion is one clear answer. In the space of fifty years (1801-51), the population of Bradford multiplied twelvefold - an increase of an incredible 1170%. By contrast, the general population of England and Wales grew in the same fifty years from nine to twenty-one million, an increase of 130%. Thus the growth of Bradford was more than ten times the national average. Even among the industrial towns of northern England, where population growth was largely concentrated, Bradford's increase is more than double that of its contemporaries.

	1801	1851	Increase
Bradford	8 525	103 778	1 170%
Salford	13 611	85 108	525%
Preston	11 887	69 542	485%
Manchester	70 409	316 213	349%
Burnley	3 305	14 706	344%
Oldham	12 024	52 820	332%
Huddersfield	7 268	30 880	324%
Leeds	53 162	172 023	223%
Wigan	10 989	31 941	190%
Wakefield	8 131	16 989	108%

Population growth in northern England, 1801-1851

A little caution must be introduced, as boundary changes and different rates of industrial development have to be taken into account. Nevertheless, Bradford's population growth was remarkable. What attracted people in such large numbers to what was, at the start of the nineteenth century, a market town situated in a dead-end valley, relatively remote from the main transport links? Arguably, it was the exploitation of coal and ironstone lying in accessible seams forty yards beneath the surface which facilitated Bradford's industrial expansion.

While the exchange of coal for Craven limestone aided the development of chemical and iron industries, it placed tremendous strain on the road network. Records for 1768 show that getting on for fifty thousand loads of coal travelled from Bradford to Skipton in that year alone. Although Bradford was by the mid-eighteenth century well connected to the turnpike road network, an alternative means of transportation became an economic and practical necessity.

A canal, the main arterial routes for heavy goods before the coming of the railways, was proposed, with its promoters claiming that they could deliver coal at one-eighth of that charged by road hauliers and half the cost of carrying limestone. Although initially the canal's raison d'être was the localised exchange of coal and limestone, the promoters saw the merits of linking the canal to the Aire and Calder Navigation at Leeds, and thence to Hull and the continent. In the opposite direction, the Aire Gap offered the opportunity of linking the canal with Liverpool and the Atlantic trade. The coal and limestone traffic that accounted for two fifths of the canal's income in 1792 rose in the ensuing three decades to become half its income by 1820. Given those figures it is perhaps unsurprising that until 1850 the headquarters of the Leeds & Liverpool Canal Company was in Bradford.

The canal was an effective conveyor of heavy bulky raw materials and its opening facilitated the expansion of several industries. The canal exported castings from the Bowling and Low Moor ironworks, flagstones from many quarries, most notably at Bolton Woods, and vitriol from chemical works on Valley Road. The ironworks produced a huge range of products: fire grates for domestic use, machinery for textile mills, and cannons that saw action at Trafalgar, Waterloo and the Crimea. The quarries situated in the hills around Bradford sold not much short of half a million tons of stone during the 1870s. It was used in numerous high profile buildings including Liverpool's Custom House and Manchester Town Hall.

However, it was the textile trade that would define Bradford. A combination of three factors carried Bradford from market town to 'worstedopolis'. Firstly, Bradford's wool and worsted products suited the market as they were serviceable cloths and were sold cheaply and in bulk. Secondly, the marketing of the finished material by local merchants, who specialised in the product and actively sought new markets, was an important contrast to the Norfolk and West Country cloth that was handled by London merchants for whom wool was one of many products. Thirdly, Bradford's proximity to other industrial towns made the textile trade responsive and receptive to change and technical innovation.

The exponential growth of the textile trade is illustrated by the fact that in 1801 there was a solitary mill in the town, while forty years later there were sixty-seven. Similarly in 1815 there were only two 'stuff' (a generic term for woven fabrics) merchants, while by 1893 there were two hundred and fifty-two. In 1835 around six thousand people were employed in the mills; by 1850 this had risen to five and a half times that number. Production underwent a similarly dramatic expansion. By 1850, thirteen times more wool was being devoured by the mills than forty years previously in 1810.

The rapid expansion of the worsted trade was once again placing a huge strain on Bradford's transport links. The canal was unable to accommodate the output with the result that much of the piece trade (fabrics sold in standard lengths) was transported by road to Leeds. By 1830 such was the volume of traffic it proved impossible to maintain the surface of the turnpike. The economic imperative of a railway connection became irresistible. It was claimed that it cost as much to transport wool by road from Bradford to Leeds (roughly nine miles) as it did to take it by rail from Leeds to Hull (fifty-eight miles). It was said that using rail to transport the large quantities of stone sent to Goole docks would result in a 50%

saving. The iron works consumed 33,000 tons of limestone annually. It was thought that an unbroken railway connection had the potential to reduce transportation costs by 2,500% per annum. Hence on 30th May 1846 the Leeds & Bradford railway line was opened, followed in 1850 by a line from Halifax and the so-called 'short-line' from Leeds in 1852. Now linked by canal, rail and road, Bradford's entrepreneurs took full advantage, with increased production right across the industrial base.

But what of the people, in all this? Grafting took on a whole new meaning as the new industries propelled the masses into mines and mills. It has often been assumed that working hours for the lower orders were so long and arduous in the latter part of the eighteenth century that opportunities for leisure were almost non-existent.

There is, however, firm evidence that life was not only about toil. Another revolution was apparently going on alongside the industrial one. By about the 1840s, Bradford's pubs were staging prize-fights, dog-fights, quoits and 'brasses', wrote one William Scruton. He also described the Bradford Fair, which took place around the Bowling Green Inn. The streets were lined with stalls and it was *a glorious medley [of] wild beast shows, waxwork exhibits, and the booths of wandering thespians, [...] conjuring ponies, fortune telling pigs, sea monsters and all the [...] fun of the fair.*

Another commentator, John James, relates that during the latter part of the eighteenth century, leisure in the town included pleasure-boating on the Bradford Canal, rowing, two 'much frequented' bowling greens at Tyrrel Street and Spink Well House, and a cockpit and bullring at the bottom of Westgate. In the very centre of the town was the 'Turls', an open space where Bradford's Town Hall stands today, which was flanked by two public houses, The Bull's Head and the Fighting Cocks, whose names themselves evidence the leisure interests of Bradfordians as the process of industrialisation and urbanisation got underway in earnest.

Interestingly, attitudes towards blood sports underwent a sea-change during the nineteenth century and events such as bull baiting and cock fighting were edged from their town centre position towards the margins of society. The formation of the Society for the Prevention of Cruelty to Animals in 1824, allied to its receipt of royal patronage in 1840 (when it became the Royal Society for the Prevention of Cruelty to Animals – today's RSPCA), was a key element in the decline of blood sports, though it was far from a complete eradication. Blood sports persisted, albeit covertly and illegally.

But the quarter-century after 1830 was a highly significant time. The official action against blood sports plus the eradication of events such as football on the public highway coincided with the spread of the railways, a rise in the disposable income of the working-class, and the staging of formalised sporting events. This twenty-five year period saw the beginning of the shift towards a modern sporting landscape.

The horse races at the Quarry Gap are significant in Bradford's sporting history as early examples of large-scale attendance at sporting events, and demonstrate the emergence of the publican as an entrepreneur of entertainment. There is undoubtedly a cultural link between the seasonal horse-race meetings and annual fairs, where socially mixed crowds would spend money carefully saved for the occasion. The seasonal nature of such meetings owed to the fact that the local population did not at that time have sufficient disposable income to have made a series of meetings financially viable. Descriptions of a one-and-three-quarter miles steeplechase staged at Quarry Gap in the spring of 1844 fit perfectly into that framework. The event attracted a mixed audience, with the Bradford Observer newspaper reporting that 'the gay blade quaffed his champagne while the sportsman of humbler pretensions was content with his brown stout'.

Frustratingly there is a paucity of evidence of whether further races were regularly taking place after the 1844 event. Not until 1855 do we see, printed in the Bradford Observer, a rather snooty response to a handbill advertising horse racing at Quarry Gap, describing it as 'remarkable for the freedom of its style, the writer having evidently disdained to be shackled by the ordinary rules of grammar'. To demonstrate this, the handbill was quoted at length:

It having been commonly the observation of travellers that Bradford is far behind the generality of towns in recreation and amusement ... a band of spirited gentlemen unite ... to light up the hearts of its toiling and industrious inhabitants once a year, in the character of horse races, on a scale not hitherto attempted in this part of the country.

An estimated twenty thousand people attended the first day's racing. The assertion that Bradford was 'far behind' other towns in staging such events could easily have been an advertising ploy rather than a statement of fact. Whether the large attendance was a desperate public flocking to an all too rare event, or evidence of a thriving sporting culture, is unknowable.

Available leisure time and the growth of the railway network were crucial for the profitability of these localised meetings. Advertisements for the Quarry Gap races informed prospective attendees that the course was a five-minute walk from Laisterdyke railway station. However, the railway could also take potential customers away from the race meetings. The Manchester Guardian, commenting on the 1845 Whitsuntide holiday, noted 'larger numbers leaving Manchester rather than spending the holidays in the traditional way at the Kersal Moor races'. It was estimated that one hundred and fifty thousand people used the railways that holiday to visit a wide range of attractions, but in particular they went to the emerging seaside resorts.

The growing trend towards formalised horse racing tracks and the suppression of the informal was consolidated when, in 1853, a new Betting Act came into force. From this time on, horse races were the only place where cash betting was legal. This resulted in the annual (until 1877) Bradford Moor races becoming notorious for heavy drinking, gambling and frequent outbreaks of fighting. A further factor facilitating what was a huge growth in illegal off-course betting was the spread of the electric telegraph. James Burnley, writing in The Yorkshireman about street scenes in 1879 Bradford, observed that *on race days the region around the Nags Head [...] a concourse of betting men is to be seen waiting the arrival of the telegraphic news [...] It is a somewhat curious fact that Bradford, remote as it is from all racing centres, should nevertheless have raised such a horde of men.*

The anti-social behaviour and illegality of the horse-racing scene prompted the centralisation of racing into purpose-built tracks. The problem of Bradford Moor races was dealt with when Bradford Corporation, in an overt display of rational recreation, purchased the site and developed Bradford Moor Park. The wild and untamed was thus replaced, in both landscape and social terms, by the formalised and rational.

But what was the fate of those who had been facilitators of the early gambling, from cockpits and bullrings to horse racing - Bradford's opportunity-seizing publicans?

2
Publicans - the entertainment entrepreneurs

Since time immemorial the pub has been an unofficial centre for sporting events and meetings. Throughout the 1850s and 1860s, as society became more urban, official pressure was brought to bear on what might be termed 'traditional sports'. Rather than leaving them to wither on the vine, they were consequently embraced by publicans. In fields adjacent to pubs, sporting grounds appeared.

These grounds, perhaps especially the one at the Quarry Gap Inn over in east Bradford, helped to preserve and shelter an older popular sporting culture within a new setting. This was an important and often overlooked moment in the development of a commercialised sporting culture. Although the sports being held would not stand the test of time, the concept of an enclosed sporting ground with gate-money and regular meetings would remain with sport for a century and a half to come.

Although gate-money was a well-established element of the sporting scene, the enclosing of grounds alongside public houses in an urban environment was a significant new development. Prior to the 1870s, publicans were thus able to reinvent themselves as 'entrepreneurs of entertainment'. These individuals were beginning to take advantage of the commercial opportunities offered by workers' new set times away from the workplace (the result of regularised working hours). Although publicans were often themselves small-time businessmen, they had a profound effect on the development of working-class leisure.

Were there women publicans? It can be safely assumed there were, but no women's names appear in the early records of those engaged with sporting and betting events. However, behind every male landlord mentioned, there would very likely have been a landlady playing her part in the running of the business.

One of the cohort of (male) 'entrepreneurs of entertainment' was Alfred Hardy, a publican in his early forties whose arrival at the Quarry Gap Inn coincided with an expansion of sporting attractions being staged in the pub and its adjacent field. Hardy gave the field the eye-catching title of the City Sporting Grounds. Large stakes were advertised to give the contests an air of theatre and confrontation. Examples staged in 1863 included a £100 knur and spell match and a foot race for £50 over one hundred and twenty yards. Apparently there was considerable betting on the outcome of both events.

Crowds were not simply tempted by potential monetary gains; they could also be attracted by curiosity to events that verged on freak-shows. In 1863 a cricket match took place between Greenwich pensioners, all minus an arm, and Chelsea pensioners, each with only one leg. The players, preceded by a brass band, were paraded in a publicity stunt around Bradford in an omnibus. The team named 'One Leg' won by fifty-one runs. The Bradford Observer reported that 'the movements of both parties were often very ludicrous, and excited roars of laughter'.

A combination of local or regional rivalry was another method of attracting a gate-paying crowd, a good example being an 1866 a cricket match between 'United South of England' and 'The Quarry Gap and District' teams. The series of cricket matches staged at Quarry Gap throughout that and the preceding year begins to illustrate an important shift in the focus of sporting leisure. The games involved a team named the 'Bradford Tailors', and took place on the growing 'Saturday half-holiday' – a newly evolving period of weekly leisure time that was being gained in an incremental fashion by different categories of workers. When, in October 1865, the Tailors met the Printers, the Bradford Observer noted that it was 'thanks to the Saturday half-holiday movement [that] these two trades were enabled to play a friendly game'. Although the Tailors disappear from Quarry Gap after 1866, this is one of the first records of the classic Saturday afternoon sporting events that have become part of our culture. It is early evidence of how spectator sports would begin to change the way people consumed their leisure time.

Team sports were not the only attraction. 'Pedestrianism' was the term used for the nowadays oft-forgotten face of Victorian professional working class athletics. Its fall into obscurity was probably due to the success of the Olympic games and its ethos of amateurism, which marginalised the older professional tradition. Pedestrianism - a catch-all term for athletics that included sprinting, endurance races, walking and leaping - had a culture and an atmosphere more akin to the prize fight or horse racing. When the Highways Act of 1835 drove Pedestrianism off the streets, the publicans welcomed this competitive athletics with open arms and became almost its sole administrators, for it was popular and profitable. Spectators paid admission money, often to a field adjacent to a public house, where bookmakers were on hand to take bets. Of course, alcohol was a staple ingredient of such events.

For publicans, staging pedestrianism events not only increased sales of alcohol; they also received commission on betting and gate receipts. The sport rapidly comprehended the link between publicity, regularity and profit. Interestingly, many pedestrianism events, even in the north of England and Scotland, were organised through the pages of the weekly newspaper Bell's Life in London. The press, in particular the weeklies, effectively facilitated, and gave birth to, a national sporting culture. Individuals may have utilised the sporting press to publicise events, slipping them in as unpaid advertisements by pretending to be bulletins on a pedestrian's progress. The challenges printed in the newspaper illustrate a high degree of professionalism. By offering prize money and handicaps, the competitors must have been acutely aware of the strengths and weaknesses of their potential opponents. Witness this typical challenge from 1852:

HARRY WATSON of Bradford will run any of the following one mile, for £25 a side, viz, Ely Parkin of Huddersfield, Rant of Holmfirth, Cob Heaton of Netherton, Jonathon Bincliffe of Raistrick, or give Pummell of Manningham 15 yards, or Gallick of Horton 30 yards in a mile. Matches can be made by sending £5 to us, and articles to the Beckett's Arms, Bradford.

Virtually all of the challenges were issued using a public house as the point of contact. Quite clearly, the Quarry Gap Inn had become part of a network of venues which utilised sporting events in order to maximise profits. In August 1862 around fifteen hundred spectators were attracted to an athletics event entitled 'English Champions'. The title was somewhat misleading as the star attraction was Louis 'Deerfoot' Bennett, an American Indian, who was advertised as 'standing five feet eleven inches in height' (this was an era when the average male height was only five feet five inches). The races were staged in the 'Deerfoot Travelling Race Course', a one thousand foot tent which enclosed a two hundred and twenty yard track. The promoter George Martin, landlord of the Royal Oak, Newton Heath, Manchester, which boasted its own race course, took the event on a nationwide tour. Undoubtedly there will have been profit-sharing of the gate receipts, and Martin even had a stake in the sale of photographs of Deerfoot which were hung in public houses all over Britain; a cult of celebrity adding to the profits of a highly commercial operation.

The Quarry Gap's most notable pedestrianism event commenced in September 1864 when local woman Emma Sharp attempted to walk one thousand miles in one thousand hours on a one hundred and twenty yard course. She walked for two miles at a time and rested every second hour. There was heavy betting and it was reported that some spectators attempted to trip her up after dark, and even that her food was doped. The event was kept in the public eye with regular announcements, such as one day's gate money, eight pounds and seventeen shillings, being donated to Bradford Infirmary. In October 1864, after fourteen thousand six hundred laps of the circuit, she completed the thousand miles in front of a reported, albeit improbable, twenty-five thousand spectators. The Bowling Brass Band led her to the finish line. A firework display, cannon fire and a roasted sheep helped along the celebrations. Emma received 'at least £500' as her share of the admission money - and used the windfall to establish a hearth-rug business!

How come it was a woman who carried out this feat? The pedestrianism scene of that period is packed full of oddities, and it was probably the case that a woman undertaking such an arduous task would have been far more eye-catching than a man. This would have enhanced the event's attraction for those paying to attend and for the betting fraternity. As for Emma herself, she was thought to have been inspired by reports of an Australian woman who had attempted a similar challenge. It is reported that her husband John attempted to talk her out of it, and was said to be so embarrassed by the attention that he hid in the pub until the crowds had melted away.

However strange pedestrianism may appear, it ought to be recognised that these often overlooked events at locations such as the Quarry Gap are a vital part of the history of athletics. Sufficient credit has not been given to entrepreneurs such as Alfred Hardy for laying the foundations of the modern athletic meeting. However, pedestrianism itself was destined to fade in the face of the Amateur Athletics Club's growing national authority, and of concerns about the influence of gambling on the legitimacy of pedestrianism races.

Another sporting oddity, at least in modern eyes, is the game of 'knur and spell' – the playing of which was simplicity itself. Individual players struck a marble-sized ball with a long-handled bat in an open field. The player who hit the ball furthest was the winner. The heartland of this historic northern English game was the West Riding of Yorkshire and into east Lancashire.

Knur and spell's name and culture links back not only to Britain's pre-industrial society, but reaches into the very fabric of northernness. It has been claimed that the game's origin hails from the northern Scandinavian bat-and-ball game *nurspell*. Players of knur and spell were often called 'laikers', which may be linked to the old Norse word *leika* which translates as 'to play'. If the actual game is simplistic, gaining access to the equipment to play is another matter. The bats, spring traps and balls were never available off-the-shelf. Apart from the 'pot knurs' (the balls), all of the equipment had to be, often painstakingly, homemade. This element of inaccessibility partly explains why the game remained at the margins of sport.

The 'stick', or bat, comprised a head with a face a few inches wide attached to a four to six foot long handle. The latter was very flexible, being fashioned from ash. The manufacture of the heads was the most closely guarded secret among players. The face was hardened by weeks of compression in specially made presses. The length of the process would vary according to the type required: a hard face for a calm day in order to punch the ball through the air; a soft face for breezy days when players would attempt to take advantage of the wind. Leading exponents of the game would arrive with a variety of 'sticks' and would select the most appropriate with the aid of a 'baumer', or caddy, to use golfing parlance. The balls were called 'knurs' and, until the 1890s, were of carved wood, around an inch and a half in diameter and dimpled in a similar fashion to a golf ball. During the late Victorian period the knur was developed into a 'pottie' – a marble-sized ball fired in a kiln from china clay. The other piece of equipment, which completes the name of the game, is the 'spell'. This was a spring trap that threw the ball into the air in order for the player to strike it. The spell perhaps epitomises knur and spell itself: incomprehensible to those unfamiliar with the game, it was an intricately-engineered piece of equipment whose mastery was almost an art, known only to the initiates.

Ideally the field needed be of fairly short grass to assist in finding knurs, and around four hundred yards in length in order to accommodate the longest of strikes. There were two main variants: 'long knock', whereby the single longest distance achieved won, or 'laikin', where every strike counted towards an overall aggregate score.

A 'laikin' scorecard from an 1863 match at the Quarry Gap
Contestant 1: Joseph Pearson, Farsley

Rises	Scores					Totals
First five	10	8	9	9	10	46
Second five	8	8	8	9	9	42
Third five	10	9	10	9	9	47
Fourth five	8	9	9	9	8	43
Fifth five	7	10	8	10	11	46
Sixth five	12	10	10	9	13	54
					Total	278

Contestant 2: James Coward, Baildon

Rises	Scores					Totals
First five	11	9	11	7	10	48
Second five	8	9	6	10	5	38
Third five	10	8	10	9	9	46
Fourth five	9	9	9	10	9	46
Fifth five	10	10	10	10	9	49
Sixth five	10	11	10	11	8	50
					Total	277

The game was played over thirty rises, a rise being the number of occasions the player attempted to strike the ball. The strikes were measured in scores of yards, hence 'ten' equals two hundred yards. The Quarry Gap match of 1863 was desperately close, and was won with the last strike of the game.

Knur and spell matches were culturally close to their folk origins, yet at its most competitive level, knur and spell had strong elements of commercialisation: many of the promoters were publicans, and there were close links with gambling. High-profile matches could reach five-figure attendances.

The survival of knur and spell into the inter-war period is a clear indication that pre-modern sport did not immediately wither on the vine once codified sports began to attract attendances in the tens of thousands. Without doubt, there was a notable transformation of popular sport between the mid-nineteenth century and the outbreak of the Great War. However, we see from the evidence of pedestrianism and of knur and spell that large crowds and commercialism were part of the sporting scene in the era before spectatorship of codified sports became widespread.

And what of the publicans? Certainly in the period before the 1870s, after which brewers began to take control of the public houses, these convivial entrepreneurs, often with sports facilities on lands adjacent to their establishments, were central figures as purveyors of the nation's sporting entertainment.

3
Workers and women: cricket's segregations

In the half-century ensuing from the 1836 formalisation of Bradford Cricket Club, cricket in Bradford was played out against a backdrop of enormous political and social change. In 1880 the grandiose development of the club's Park Avenue home would ultimately force the club to embrace aspects of commercialism in order to finance the ground.

Across Bradford the appeal of cricket widened as more workers began to be granted the Saturday half-holiday. What we know today as 'the weekend' was beginning to appear, and cricket was at the vanguard of that change.

In the political arena, throughout the 1830s and 1840s the largely Anglican Tories and Nonconformist Liberals were fighting for control of Bradford. Meanwhile the new working class movement of Chartism was rising, and from 1838 came to dominate British politics for the subsequent decade.

The worker-friendly aims of the Chartists were: universal suffrage, annual elections, equally divided electoral districts, payment of MPs, abolition of the property qualification for MPs, and vote by secret ballot. Booming Bradford with its seething masses of exploited workers emerged as a heartland of the so-called 'physical force Chartists'.

The incorporation of the town in 1847 was a pivotal moment, signalling the beginning of the domination of local politics by the Liberals for half a century. Despite the still-restricted franchise, Bradford's politicians were deeply aware of the influence of the working classes on elections: there were street demonstrations and boycotts of businesses, and the famous violent Chartist risings of 1840, 1842 and 1848.

Richard Oastler's campaign, highlighting the plight of children's working conditions in mills, was an attempt to forge an alliance between the Tories and the working class. Oastler's denunciation of the factory system and his evocation of a harmonious semi-rural golden age, where the pace of work was leisurely and deference was the unspoken foundation, resonated with handloom weavers who faced redundancy as mechanisation spread. However, as the Tories refused to support voting rights for the working classes, Oastler's campaign split, rather than galvanised, Bradford's working class reformers.

Between 1850 and 1860 the population of Bradford grew by only three thousand but the value of property increased exponentially during this period. The scale of development can be discerned from the number of plans deposited with Bradford Corporation. In the years 1850 and 1854, plans were received for upwards of two hundred new streets and six and a half thousand new buildings, including one hundred and thirteen warehouses and mills. As wealth grew, Bradford entered its 'great period'. A commercial treaty with France in 1860, negotiated by the Bradford wool merchant Jacob Behrens, led to a decade of continuous growth. It reached its peak in 1872 when woollen and worsted materials, worth a staggering forty million pounds, were exported from Bradford to overseas markets.

As mechanisation of the textile industry spread, the number of hand-combers and weavers declined steeply. This, allied to the relative prosperity of the 1850s, fatally undermined Chartism. Activists forged links with middle-class non-conformists such as the immensely wealthy mill-owners Titus Salt and W.E. Forster. Thus, in the mid-nineteenth century, the foundations of popular Liberalism and the 'respectable working class' were laid.

Cricket was being played throughout this era. Inevitably, the process of industrialisation was to reshape 'the nation's favourite game'. The movement of working hours towards the 'factory system' (essentially, the mechanisation of production in a centralised location, plus the introduction of set working hours), coupled with the expansion of the town of Bradford, were two factors in this.

During the early 1830s, cricket matches were taking place quite extensively within the Bradford district, with some being staged at rural locations on the fringes of the town on common land. It could be surmised that the playing of matches on the edge of the town was a response to rapid urbanisation and a difficulty of finding suitable land on which to play, or it may have been the case that playing on common land was an easy option for teams who appear to have been fairly informal in their organisation.

The 1836 formalisation of Bradford Cricket Club was a significant development: it appears to be the first time in Bradford's sporting history that a sports club was somewhat recognised for its function as a representative of the city. During its early years, the cricket club was dominated by the town's Anglican Tory elite. It was also of course a man's domain, and highly class-conscious. Initially the club had no settled home ground. However, in 1839 the club secured a field adjacent to Mannville, home of the textile family the Manns who were patrons of the club.

Bradford's matches were played on Mondays and Tuesdays, and attendances in the low thousands suggest that the disciplining of workers was not as effective as it would become. Prior to the introduction of large-scale machine-powered industry, work was often task-based rather than time based, and within such a structure, the working day could be shortened or lengthened. Before the standardisation of the working week, some, mostly skilled, workers would absent themselves from work on a Monday if finances allowed it. This casual extension of Sunday became known as Saint Monday. Indeed, an 1842 children's employment commission report stated that in Bradford, Monday was chiefly spent by adults drinking or recovering from the effects of it.

The facilities Bradford Cricket Club was developing could be utilised for public spectacles, with attendant profits. The use of cricket grounds for ancillary events appears to have been fairly common, both as a valuable income stream and a way of cementing the club's image as a central part of the civic identity. One such event was a 'great pyrotechnic fete' held in 1844. Alongside the fireworks a balloon race was planned, and the Bradford Temperance Brass Band was to play. An advertisement announcing the admission prices, and entry arrangements, is a mix of commercialism and social segregation. Ladies and gentlemen were to be charged sixpence, with entrance at the top gate; working people and children thrupence, with entrance by the lower gate. A space was allocated for carriages from where the occupants could witness the display 'without alighting'.

As said, the club was dominated by a Tory elite. Hence the club's 1844 annual dress ball was patronised by Lord John Manners, Tory MP for Newark and leading light in Disraeli's 'Young England' movement, who was touring industrial districts in that year to advocate for public holidays, factory reform and the allotment system.

Other wealthy Tory worthies in attendance were listed as Wm. Busfeild Ferrand, Esq., the Bingley born Tory MP for Knaresborough; Captain Thomas H. Horsfall of Hawksworth Hall; Joshua Mann Esq., a stuff merchant and chairman of the Bradford Subscription concerts and whose family owned Mannville House adjacent to the cricket ground; his brother John Mann Esq. of Boldshay Hall, and Joshua Pollard JP, a Tory councillor.

Anticipating the ball, the Bradford Observer reflected on the achievements of the cricket club, describing its ethos as *amusement to all classes [...] the creation of a spirit of emulation in other clubs, by selecting the best men in the neighbourhood to practice with and take part in matches [...] the Bradford Cricket Club had thus witnessed springing up around them a large number of clubs [...] the club numbers about 150 subscribers, including the elite of our gentry. It is gratifying thus to be able to trace the establishment, growth, and history of such a society, which appears to have kept pace with the wants of the times, and when mills and manufacturers are making such rapid growth, participation in healthy amusements tend generally to improve the physical and mental condition of society.*

The overt Tory backing of the local cricket club was probably a deliberate identification with outdoor popular culture designed to distance the Conservatives from the Liberal moral reformists. In one instance it was claimed that the strongly non-conformist Liberals, with links to the Temperance Movement, would 'rob the British workman of his beer'. This stance would help define politics in the popular imagination until at least the turn of the century, and became vital to Conservative electoral success in the wake of the 1867 enfranchisement of urban working class voters.

At the end of the 1851 season, Bradford's mid-century building boom resulted in the cricket ground being sold for the construction of substantial middle-class villas. The road serving the villas was named Claremont. In 1860 the composer Frederick Delius, whose father was a German born wool merchant, was born at number 6 Claremont. The cricket club moved to a field behind Claremont, barely an off-drive from their former home. Living adjacent to the cricket ground perhaps explains Delius's lifelong love of the game. However, the 1860s and 1870s saw Bradford Cricket Club decline to the brink of extinction. In 1861 the Bradford Observer lamented the decline in numbers of gentlemen players and the fact that unless younger players emerged, the club would 'lose its proud position in the cricketing world'.

The cricket club identified that a way of improving the club's finances would be to organise an athletics festival. Such events were an established part of the Victorian sporting calendar, and athletes would travel across the country to take part in the festivals. Bradford Cricket Club's first athletics festival was held in July 1869. Between three and four thousand spectators enjoyed fourteen events, including hammer throwing, hurdling, shot-putting, walking and running races. Six gold medals, two silver cups, fourteen silver medals and fourteen bronze medals were competed for. By the time of the club's fifth annual athletic festival in July 1873 the club appears to have become reliant on the profits of the festival in order to remain solvent. The 1873 festival earned the club one hundred and fifty pounds and ten shillings, which equates to 14.5% of the club's income for the year. Without the windfall, the club would have lost thirty-six pounds, two shillings and eightpence.

The elitism of the club was still in place in 1869, prompting the Bradford Observer to accuse the club of being 'too much of a gentlemen's association'. The article insisted that it was essential that the cricket club should adopt a meritocratic approach, arguing that it might then be in a position to 'uplift once more the reputation of Bradford cricket'. Such sentiments were perhaps the inevitable conclusions of a liberal newspaper. Working class players were indeed increasingly dominating northern club cricket, and socially elite clubs would struggle against clubs that were truly meritocratic.

Bradford's situation was made all the more perilous because its home ground was again in danger of being converted into highly desirable plots of building land. The sale of the Horton Hall estate in 1871 set in train a series of events that would witness Little Horton develop as a gentrified area for the growing middle class. Sir Francis Sharp Powell MP purchased plots at Ashgrove and

Pemberton Drive - the site of the cricket ground. The influence of Powell on the development and character of the Little Horton area is crucial. The Tory MP inherited the Horton Green estate in 1844. Despite many 'tempting offers', he kept his estate as a green oasis among the rapidly expanding city. The covenant he placed on the development of Little Horton ensured that middle-class villas were constructed.

So in October 1874, the final match at Horton Road was played. The club was then in limbo as sites for a new ground were evaluated. None proved to be viable, which led the club committee to recommend that the club be wound up. That attracted a spate of letters to the Bradford Observer, one of which suggested that the club should merge with Manningham Cricket Club who, the writer claimed, had 'drawn away much of the best young blood' and that the 'increase in land rents and reduction in the number of Horton supporters' had fatally undermined Bradford Cricket Club. Another correspondent thought that if money and aristocratic influence were essential elements for the successful running of a cricket club then Manningham was the 'most preferable place'. The reference to 'Horton' possibly illustrates the competition between the middle class suburbs of Horton and Manningham for the cultural soul of the growing city. Another letter claimed that Bradford Cricket Club was much more than being a merely 'private' club and that the club was 'to all intents and purposes the town's club'. The writer concluded by stating that a cricket club was as important to a large town as 'public baths or public parks'.

For a full five years Bradford Cricket Club remained dormant until, in 1879, a fourteen-year lease of land adjacent to Horton Park was at last signed, facilitating the construction of a joint cricket and rugby ground. The latter would accommodate Bradford Rugby Club. A public subscription attempted to raise the £4,000 required for the development. Although the dominant sports would be cricket and rugby, facilities for lawn tennis, archery and quoits were provided. In order to both finance the development and ensure its future viability, the cricket club merged in 1880 with Bradford Rugby Club, and the resulting body was named the Bradford Cricket, Athletic & Football Club (BCA & FC). The football in the title referred to the rugby club because the Victorians, confusingly to modern eyes, continued to call rugby 'football' long after the emergence of the round ball game.

Grand ambitions for the Park Avenue grounds can be detected by the facilities: there were two pavilions, with the lower of the two having frontages onto both the cricket and rugby pitches, whilst the main pavilion at the top of the ground boasted a refreshment bar behind a near one hundred and thirty foot long balcony.

Was the cricket ethos fundamentally more inclusive of women, at least as spectators, than rugby football? Certainly the style of spectatorship was - and is to this day - typically more peaceful and civilised than the roaring and reportedly foul-mouthed crowds at rugby matches. It is of note that the new-built eastern and western wings of Park Avenue's facilities housed a ladies' cloak room along with the dressing rooms and committee room, serving hypothetically both rugby and cricket attendees.

Whether these toilets would have been, in practice, accessible to all women attendees is another matter. The facilities demonstrate Victorian social segregation. The separations within pavilions, grandstands, balconies and dining facilities, and price segregation of different parts of the ground, were common at virtually every large-scale county cricket ground.

As to women taking part in cricket as players: the evolution of women's participation in any spectator sport in Bradford was generally both delayed and sidelined in the face of 'male' spectator sports culture. Hence the story of women in this sphere falls into a later époque than this tale is able to cover. In brief, looking nationwide, women were first recorded as playing cricket in the mid-1700s, in southern English villages and small towns. Yorkshire folk may find it gratifying that the first actual women's cricket club was indeed a Yorkshire one: the 'White Heather Club' at Nun Appleton, founded in 1887. However, in the Bradford context, there was little action for women cricketers until well into the twentieth century, when the Hey's Ladies' Cricket Club was formed (1925) out of workers from the Hey's Brewery on Lumb Lane in Manningham - after a short history of being a football team!

At last, on 20th July 1880, the ambitiously renovated grounds of Park Avenue were declared open by the Lord Mayor of Bradford – a significant moment, since the presence of the mayor sent a clear message that Park Avenue was recognised as part of the civic infrastructure on a par with the public parks and St. George's Hall. Park Avenue was a status symbol that resonated beyond the sporting. The decorative pavilions and attendant sports represented respectability. Following a match between Gentlemen and Players, dinner was served in the pavilion. The Mayor toasted the health of the Queen, various members of the Royal family and the army, navy and volunteer forces. Among the guests were officers of the 103rd Regiment.

Of national significance was the speech made at the opening by Lieutenant-Colonel Frankland. Overt associations were drawn between the new sports venue, the civic elite and the imperial mission of sport, at the same time as an expression of regret for the unsatisfactory state of the army:

He felt he was addressing the intelligent population of one of our most important manufacturing towns, who had an influence in the voice of the nation [...] he hoped that this important question would meet with the attention of Parliament and the nation at large [...] he concluded by proposing the health of the Bradford Cricket, Athletic and Football Club

[...] and the importance of young men going in for athletics [...] He spoke warmly of his appreciation of outdoor sports, and of cricket in particular. He compared favourably our physical condition with that of Continental nations, and ascribed the cause to the English love of athletics.

Thus, by the day the first ball was bowled, a link between cricket and the military had already been firmly established. As early as 1841 the commander-in-chief of the army ordered the preparation of a cricket ground as close as possible to every army barracks in the country. This greatly aided the establishment of cricket as the national game and raised its social standing. Arthur Thompson, writing in his beautiful book 'Odd Men In, a gallery of cricket eccentrics', imagined an invisible thread connecting the industrial greensward at Park Avenue with the exotica of Empire when he wrote of soldiers and cricketers, *both need courage and endurance; both are skilled in adapting themselves without warning to various forms of sticky wicket, as in Burma or even Bradford Park Avenue.*

Rugby kicked off to an ignominious start at the Park Avenue ground, the first match being staged in September 1880 with Bradford being defeated by Bradford Rangers. Though it was reported that the game attracted considerable interest, the fanfare of the opening cricket match was absent. Yet despite this low-key beginning, rugby would in time become the financially dominant aspect of the BCA & FC and would subsidise the cricket.

Cricket's self-image, as constructed by generations of writers and commentators, makes innumerable references to pastoral England (shorthand for the home counties) – the vision of the squire, parson and farm labourer playing on the village green. This image was vigorously consumed by the urban middle class, seeking escapism from industrialisation and modernity via Arcadian descriptions of the countryside of which cricket was an integral part. Even when played in heavily industrialised locales, cricket often conjured the same image of temporal and spatial conformity in which the various forms and manifestations of the game were the same, the ultimate form being the mythic rural cricket field: timeless, pastoral and with a natural social hierarchy. Perhaps this can help explain why cricket's importance as one of the first team sports adopted by industrial workers as the Saturday half-holiday began to spread has often been overlooked.

The first step towards giving the working class a structured time to play and watch sport came with the 1850 Factory Act, requiring mills to close on Saturday afternoons at two o'clock. Cricket at county level was now out of step with industrial urban society due to its failure to modernise. The sedate tempo of the game, often spread over several working days, was a quaint anomaly in comparison to the frantic excitement of the football codes. County cricket therefore never became an all-consuming passion for the working classes, whereas the more accessible league cricket had great appeal as a spectator sport. The cricket leagues had far more in common socially and economically with rugby and football than they did with county cricket.

In 1856 Bradford Cricket Club began staging almost weekly games between the Saturday half-holiday clubs and warehousemen. The Bradford Observer's reports of matches in the ensuing decade give us a broad picture of the development of working class cricket. A look at one representative month's reports (July, being mid-cricket-season, thus capturing the majority of teams then in existence) reveals some emergent patterns. The newspaper was reliant on correspondents submitting match details, therefore some matches may have been omitted due to pressure on space or editorial judgment; also the weather had an impact on the number of matches played. However there is clear evidence that the majority of matches in the early part of that decade were between work-based teams. Of the nine reported matches in July 1856, all were such teams, whereas by the last Saturday of July 1866, of the thirty-two teams in action only four were representing workplaces or trades, while twenty-seven were geographic.

Furthermore, the second half of the decade saw a sharp increase in the number of matches, from an average of about ten matches each July until, in 1863, a sudden leap to twenty-seven, followed by two Julys in which almost fifty matches were played, rising to a substantial total of sixty-two matches in 1866. When the first major rise happened in 1863 the newspaper started printing full scorecards for the first time, though this may represent an editorial decision to increase the coverage of cricket, rather than being a response to the sudden surge in the number of matches.

Within the seemingly humdrum world of workplace cricket there were exotic elements of internationalism, since many teams represented German-owned businesses. Bradford's small but highly influential German community transformed the distribution side of the textile business, bringing efficiency and businesslike terms of payment. Within thirty years they were fully integrated into the business and civic community. In 1864 Charles Semon, a Danzig man, became Bradford's first foreign mayor. When Jacob Behrens was knighted by Queen Victoria in 1882 it was a recognition of the centrality and importance of Bradford's German, and largely Jewish, community.

Historians have often referenced the 'high culture' interests of the German community, most notably in connection with the classical subscription concerts. The sporting interests of Bradford's Germans, such as Frederick Delius's love of cricket, are hinted at in a variety of sources, but almost always anecdotally. Another example is the poet Humbert Wolfe's autobiographical 'Now a Stranger', a description of growing up in a prosperous Jewish German-Italian household in Manningham between the 1880s and the Great War. Apparently as a boy in the gardens of the exclusive villas of Mount Royd, Wolfe played cricket.

From 1856 cricket teams of warehousemen from German-owned businesses were active. Many of the German businessmen were aware of an employer's social obligations to their workforce, so the teams may have been officially sanctioned acts of philanthropy. The assistance of clubs by these employers (S.L. Behrens, A.S. Sichel, Schunk Brothers & Co, E. Wurtzburg & Co, N. Reichemheim & Co, S. Barsdorf & Co, Kessler & Co, and Schwann, Kell & Co) may have been an endeavour to steer employees away from the temptations of the public house and thus improve productivity via a healthy and engaged workforce. However, the fact that the teams representing the German companies were composed almost entirely of players with British surnames suggests they had been formed and organised by the workers with little or no official involvement. One notable exception was Frederick Sigismund Schwann, the son of John Schwann, the German-born owner of Schwann, Kell & Co, who was third to the crease when the company played Manningham United in 1863.

Cricket was also booming away from the workplace. The neighbourhood teams, many of which began life playing on any ground that could be found and operating under an array of bizarre names, slowly transformed into formalised clubs. Permanent grounds were developed, and identification with the immediate locality began to take root. Examples of this transition include two Yeadon teams: the Topenders and the Lowenders, which emerged from cricket matches played on Saturday evenings after work on Yeadon Moor. The two teams merged in 1859 to become Yeadon United. At Idle a 'Fat Pot' club was in existence prior to formation of Idle United in 1861. They became the Idle Lillywhites in 1865, and finally Idle in 1889. At Lidget Green a team named 'T'Blazing Rag' was formed in the 1870s. By 1880 they had become Lidget Green United and a pitch had been laid at their Legrams Lane ground.

There was also a religious element to some formations. To the south of Bradford, Spen Victoria was formed in 1862 at Cleckheaton Wesleyan Chapel, while the vicar of St. Mary's formed Gomersal in 1896. By any measure, this was a notable expansion. In a handful of decades, club cricket had found its way into almost every nook and cranny of Victorian Bradford.

Whatever the inspiration for the formation of the teams, whether they sprang from the comradeship of workers or the camaraderie of residential neighbourhoods, or were initiatives within companies run by Germans of largely Jewish backgrounds, it is notable that all were playing the quintessential English game of cricket. The social diversity of Bradford cricket's early days has continued into the contemporary cricket scene in which Bradfordians of Bangladeshi, Indian and Pakistani descent have embraced and given new life to the local game.

4
The rise of rugby

The game of football has probably always been with us in one form or another. Informal games were undoubtedly played in the fields and streets of Bradford for generations. However, it was the returning sons of industrialists from their public school education that would spark nothing short of a revolution in Bradford's sporting tastes.

Although rugby was initially a sport for the elite, its appeal rapidly spread to all classes and it became by far the most popular spectator sport in late nineteenth century Bradford. The evolution of rugby into a popular, commercialised and professional sport is one of the key developments in sporting history. It wrought changes on a national and international scale that continue to resonate to this day. And Bradford was the epicentre of this evolution.

Histories of football and rugby have often given great weight to the role of the public schools in developing the games, though the rules created by institutions such as Rugby and Eton must have been formulations of games already being played in wider society. Surely rugby and football would not have spread so rapidly post-1870 without an extant and popular culture?

The earliest written reference to football in Bradford dates back three hundred years. In 1720 football was reportedly one of the sports played by the pupils of Bradford Grammar School (needless to say, a boys' school), alongside the pastimes of bowls, kites, marbles, shuttlecocks, skating and tops. Sporadic evidence of informal games of football, mainly from around the Christmas break, appear in court and crime reports in the Bradford Observer between 1838 and 1849. Reports include a youth being fined following an assault when a 'subscription ball' was snatched from a group of 'lads' playing football at Horton on Christmas Day 1838. A year later, Joseph Hepworth of Idle was charged with shooting a gun at two 'lads' who were kicking a football on his land. Near the end of the decade, the body of a child was found by boys 'kicking a football' in Water Lane, Thornton Road. A writer in the Bradford Observer could remember when 'the whole of Hall Ings revelled in green fields, and when the young and stalwart Bradfordians played football there in the winter season'.

Although these reports are few and far between, it is clear that a form of football was being played, and the game was sufficiently well known to not need explaining to newspaper readers. By the late 1850s, hints of formalised matches suggest that football had developed beyond the informal street kick-abouts into something more recognisably modern. In 1858 a letter-writer complained about the desecration of the Sabbath at Spinkwell Bridge by 'between twenty and thirty young men'. The writer believed that it was not a 'mere pastime' but was a set game; however, the casual nature of these games means no records were created.

Local politics played its part in the growth of a sporting culture. Decisions made about access to education for more of the population were to have a significant impact, in view of the crucial role of schools in introducing youth to sports.

In the mid to late nineteenth century, politics in Bradford was dominated by Liberal manufacturers, following the formation of a borough council in 1847 that had provided the platform for a Liberal political breakthrough. In the first election, Liberals won thirty-two of the forty-two seats contested; thereafter, six of the town's first seven mayors were Liberals. Three years after the formation of the borough council, an Improvement Act began a process that sought to civilise the urban environment. Issues addressed included policing, sewerage, smoke abatement and transport. These problems in the rapidly industrialising city were addressed by the Liberals in a manner that could be criticised as paternalistic, yet enough of the new so-called 'respectable working class' shared those values to make liberalism the established ideology for fifty years.

The Liberal consensus was underpinned by prosperity. However, that prosperity became less predictable from the mid-1870s when Bradford's overseas competitors began erecting trade barriers. In 1874 France introduced a 10% tariff on textile imports, with Germany following suit in 1879. A change in fashion towards soft, clinging materials, mostly made in France, was a further blow to Bradford's trade. One response to these new challenges was the opening of a technical college (1878) offering design and manufacturing education, part of its aim being to match, and surpass, the skill of foreign designers and workers.

With the decline of profits due to the foreign trade tariffs, the paternalism of the liberal manufacturers came under pressure. The consequential withdrawal of these manufacturers from some of their philanthropic initiatives began to dissolve the bonds between the workers and their employers. A revived Tory Party tapped into the resulting disconnect. The Tories' enthusiasm for imperialism proved attractive to manufacturers and workers at a time when Bradford's trade was being realigned towards the empire due to the foreign trade tariffs. The party was receiving solid support from a growing lower middle class such as shopkeepers, clerks and local government officials. They also retained working-class support that remembered Oastler's factory reforms. Such was the increase in support for Toryism that in 1892, a Conservative newspaper, the Bradford Daily Argus, was launched. The Liberals, split by Gladstone's 1886 Home Rule Bill for Ireland, could not counter their opponent's populism and in their 1895 General

Election victory, the Tories won two of the three Bradford parliamentary seats.

Although it was conceded that the 'immense fortunes' made during the 1870s would probably not be repeated, some reforms were made that aided a recovery and by 1884 Bradford's economy had largely bounced back. The Bradford Observer, reflecting on the changes, noted that while the very wealthy had suffered, smaller manufacturers and the operatives were 'wealthier than they were five years ago'.

What of sport in this period? The relative stability and progress of the mid-century had enabled a growth in sporting culture. In the pervasive atmosphere of capitalist and imperialist values, that culture's characteristics of 'competition' and 'civic identity' (shaped by the nation's wider cultural and political values), have arguably continued to be British sport's dominant ethic to this day.

It is vital in this context to look at the educational revolution that swept through the public schools in the second half of the nineteenth century, in view of schools' key role in instilling sporting values.

At mid-century, the nationwide grammar school system included a number of 'failing schools' - grossly inefficient, with low numbers of pupils - of which Bradford Grammar School happened to be a prime example. In 1864, with only forty-two boy pupils and three masters, it was in 'a very bad state'.

W.E. Forster's revolutionary Endowed Schools Act (1869) stimulated the turn-around of Bradford Grammar. Three new governors were welcomed: Jacob Behrens, a German non-conformist wool merchant; William Byles, the non-conformist editor of the liberal Bradford Observer, and Edward Ripley, the Methodist owner of an enormous dye works. All three were liberals and they transformed the governing body that since 1662 had been strictly Anglican and Tory.

The Act also opened the way for girls' schooling, and in 1875 Bradford Girls' Grammar School was founded. The school was evidently innovative and successful, and was one of the first in the country to include in its curriculum Physical Education for girls, though a gymnasium would not be built until 1927. Whatever the girl pupils' physical training entailed, there was no competitive sport in girls' education that held an equivalence to the sports of football and rugby in terms of their wider social impact.

What was the state of sports at the boys' grammar school in this period? It appears to have had a lukewarm attitude to games. In 1877 only thirty boys were reported to have been regular rugby players. Although this number grew to nearly sixty the following year (from an intake of four hundred and fifty), these were low numbers in comparison to similar institutions. Furthermore, in the subsequent year (1879) it is even on record that no sports were entered into during the winter.

When, ten years later, a subscription appeal was launched to purchase a cricket field, the school chose not to mention the fact that they also planned to lay out a rugby pitch, as 'some parents thought it a vulgar, rough game'. Julius Delius, father of the composer Frederick, was said to have been firmly of that opinion.

Of course, while many nineteenth-century industrialists were strong supporters of the public school system, not every Bradford family with the means to send their boys to fee-paying public schools concurred with the ethos of Bradford Grammar School. For those unable or unwilling to send their offspring south, there were several Yorkshire schools which had a strong games ethic.

One such establishment was Bramham College, founded in 1842-3 by the liberal non-conformist Dr Benjamin Bentley Haigh. The influence of this college on the evolution of rugby in Yorkshire cannot be overestimated. 'Muscular Christianity ... represented by notices of drill, cricket and [rugby] football' was Bramham

College's sporting ethos. The college's influence is evidenced by a rugby game against Wharfedale College at Boston Spa in 1864, when the Bramham team contained the members of the founding families of Bradford Rugby Football Club (Jack Ingham), Huddersfield RFC (Harry Beardsell), and Hull RFC (R.J. Wade).

And so to Bradford Rugby Club, formed in 1863 by young men who had been initiated into the game at their schools, including Bramham and also Steeton Hall boarding school that Bradford-born Joseph Riley founded in 1856 (after running a similar school at Benton Park, Rawdon). The club elected as leader Oates Ingham, son of the owner of Lingfield Dyeworks, who had existing ties with Bradford Cricket Club as the dyeworks band had serenaded crowds prior to matches on several occasions. It is likely that his personal ties facilitated Bradford RFC utilising the cricket club's Horton Road ground for two winters.

It says a lot about Bradford that it was the first city in Yorkshire to form a rugby club, and among the earliest countrywide, hot on the heels of Liverpool (1857), Manchester (1860) and Sale (1861). Bradford was in the sporting vanguard nationally. However, like the majority of other clubs, initially Bradford played a game that might be described as a mixture of Rugby and Association Football.

The club's earliest games were probably *ad hoc* affairs - captain's side against secretary's side; games with universities and schools – until, in 1866, with more opposition becoming available, it was decided to put in place a formal structure to facilitate an organised schedule of rugby games. Only at this moment did Bradford fully adopt the rugby game. That decision may have been a pragmatic one, in that the majority of the available opposition within a reasonable travelling distance played the rugby game, or a version close enough to it to allow an easy conversion.

But complaints came. Two seasons in, Bradford Cricket Club was concerned about damage to the pitch. So by 1874 the rugby club had moved to a new ground at Apperley Bridge, a one-minute walk from the railway station and adjacent to the Stansfield Arms. The move buoyed up the club. During the 1874-5 season they won every match, and did not concede a single point.

Or was it all down to the new captain? Harry Garnett, who took up the role in the year of the move and held it for the next seven years, is one of Yorkshire rugby's historically most influential figures - another product of the public schools. Harry's education may have been one of the explanations for Bradford playing full hacking rules, in contrast to many other northern clubs. His family, who owned a paper mill at Otley, sent him south to Blackheath Preparatory School (its pupils were to found Blackheath Rugby Club). It is very likely his school's influence made Harry one of the driving forces behind Bradford's early adoption of Rugby School rules. Simultaneously with being Bradford's captain, Harry was a committee member of the Yorkshire Rugby Union (YRU) and became YRU president in 1876, then again in 1884, and was also president of the English Rugby Union 1889-90.

Interest in rugby was now beginning to grow beyond those who had attended public schools, and business and social connections started to be a means of attracting participants. Ingham said, when questioned as to the respectability of his fledgling Bradford club, 'well, you know me and do business with my firm'. There appears to have been a growing social prestige attached to playing rugby that was absent in the older versions of football. The membership fees charged by Bradford RFC during 1868 was two shillings and sixpence, exactly the same amount as Huddersfield and Hull. As in all spheres, social class and snobbery were part of the tapestry of the rugby scene. The fees were beyond the reach of the wider population, making the early clubs socially exclusive. Initially there were few spectators, and none of the twenty-one provincial clubs listed in the 1868 *Football Annual* charged admission to their matches.

Another interesting development: the majority of clubs in Lancashire and Yorkshire had a close relationship with the textile trade, and the social and business connections built by industrialism began to be utilised to organise matches. In a way, rugby was turning into a recreational medium for municipal and trade rivalry. Then came the catalyst for a series of events that was to utterly transform the nature and face of rugby in Yorkshire and beyond: the 1877 introduction of the Yorkshire Cup competition.

Cup competitions were drivers of cultural change wherever they were played. This is especially notable with football. It has been claimed that football's first ever knock-out competition was the Sheffield Cup (1867). As a direct result of the success of the cup competition, the Sheffield Football Association formed. The Scottish Cup, inaugurated in 1873, had by its second year made football an obsession in Glasgow. The Lancashire Cup (1879), allied to the involvement, and success, of the county's clubs in the FA Cup, widened the appeal of football, and the fact that the conservative Lancashire Rugby Union refused to sanction a cup competition aided football's rapid advance in the 'red rose county' (Lancashire). By contrast, the early establishment of rugby's Yorkshire Cup probably held back the football tide for three decades in the 'white rose county' of Yorkshire (Lancashire's rival since ancient times).

Back to the inauguration of the Yorkshire Cup – with the stated aims of making rugby the game of choice for every boy in the county, and raising standards until Yorkshire could meet and defeat the rest of England. The motion was tabled by Harry Garnett and Frederick Schutt, head of a wool merchant business founded by his Hamburg-born father (another example of the involvement of second generation Germans in sport).

The cup was an immediate success, attracting large attendances to the cup-ties. Bradford's Yorkshire Cup exit, at the hands of eventual winners Wakefield Trinity in 1879, prompted a meeting of players from clubs across Bradford to consider how the strongest possible side could be fielded from the available talent within the district. Bradford RFC faced accusations of being too exclusive. The accusations of elitism appear to have been acknowledged, with captain Harry Garnett agreeing that it was 'very necessary that Bradford be better represented'. In exchange for an influx of the district's best playing talent, the club was reorganised and a new committee formed.

Although it took the reconstituted club five years to win the Yorkshire Cup (1884), it had by that time transformed itself into England's premier club, having merged with Bradford Cricket Club in 1880 and developed the Park Avenue grounds. Although this had introduced significant overheads, profits increased from £300 in 1880 to £2,000 only six years later.

The club was becoming an increasingly commercialised organisation. A combination of growing attendances, profits and competition for Yorkshire County Cricket Club matches led, at last, to the incorporation of BCA & FC in 1891. The object of the limited company was to buy the ground at a sale price of £13,000 and expand the facilities. In order to effectively compete, Bradford had no option but to function as a capitalist enterprise.

Bradford's self-image as an elite club remained a constant point of controversy, and as the crowds, and their money, poured through the Park Avenue turnstiles, the contradictions would multiply. Along with the sidelining of women in Bradford's sporting culture, class divisions simmered interminably. It is ironic that it was

Bradford's Blackheath-educated advocate of hacking, Harry Garnett, who had opened the Pandora's Box of cup rugby.

The success of the Yorkshire Cup had brought with it a democratisation of the rugby game with new players and spectators flooding in. Halifax's victory in the inaugural final possibly inspired the formation of new clubs whose social structures and ethos differed significantly from rugby's founding fathers. One such club appeared in Bradford's township of Manningham.

Was Manningham Rugby Football Club, as has often been claimed, Bradford's first 'people's team'? How true is this perception? As the ensuing account will show, Manningham RFC was a far more complex organisation than its self-image suggests.

The suburb's early development catered to a carriage-owning elite looking to escape the noise and pollution of Bradford, starting with the construction in 1832 of the splendid Bolton Royd villa of J.G. Horsfall, a spinner and worsted manufacturer. Numerous large villa residences followed. Thirty years on, middle class homes were being constructed at Peel Square, Hanover Square and Southfield Square, then the 1870s saw improved public transport that brought the suburbs within reach of the lower middle class and skilled workers, and also facilitated the industrialisation of Manningham: Drummonds Mills opened in1869; Manningham locomotive depot in 1872, and Manningham Mills in 1872-80. The final three decades of the nineteenth century saw the remaining open space fill up with lower-class terraced housing.

That 1870s influx of perhaps aspirational lower-middle-class and skilled workers coincided with Rugby's emergence in Manningham. The game is first mentioned in an 1873 advertisement in the Bradford Observer. Despite the changes in Manningham's demographics, 1870's rugby in the suburb had a middle-class profile. A club formed mid-century was a short-lived affair as the club folded in 1877, when many players gravitated towards Bradford RFC to join its quest to win civic glory for Bradford in the Yorkshire Cup.

The following year however, a new club was founded named Manningham Clarence. It looked more like a winter offshoot of Manningham Clarence Cricket Club, in that both played in Manningham Park and shared several players.

In their second season, under new name Manningham Albion, the club moved to Shipley to a new home near the Branch Hotel, thus loosening its ties with the cricket club. It now began charging spectators to watch games - a sign of increasing maturity. With an average gate income of just two shillings and ninepence, players had to cover their own incidentals and travelling expenses. A dearth of records of the cost of watching Manningham's games makes it hard to estimate the numbers of their spectators. However, in that year, association football clubs were charging between tuppence and sixpence a match. Assuming Manningham was charging the lowest possible fee - a farthing (quarter of a penny), the average number of paying spectators would have been around one hundred and thirty.

In the summer of 1880 the club moved back to Manningham, renting a ground that took its name from the adjacent Carlisle Road. The move saw regular four figure crowds attending games. On the opening day of the 1884-5 season, Manningham unveiled new claret and amber club colours. Why these colours? Given the proximity of Belle Vue barracks, it might have been that Manningham adopted the claret and amber of the local regiment - the Prince of Wales' Own (West Yorkshire). Weight is added to that theory by the dominance in the newspapers of the 1884 Sudan Campaign, and in particular the Siege of Khartoum, for Bradford's grandees were vociferous, playing their part on the national stage. Bradford MP William Forster criticised the hesitant policy of his own party and the danger to General Gordon at Khartoum. Partly due to Forster's persistence, the government eventually dispatched reinforcements to Egypt, which included the Green Howards, the sister regiment to the Belle Vue based West Yorkshire Regiment.

Even before the drama at Khartoum, regiments were becoming a source of local pride and were often a central part of civic ceremony and pageantry. By adopting the colours claret and amber, Manningham's rugby club was aspiring to the respectability and standing of the regiment. The club's association with the military dovetails with the public's growing esteem of the army, as a combination of fears of militarist European nationalism and recurrent scares of invasion took root in the national imagination.

When Manningham took up residence at Carlisle Road in 1880 the surrounding land was fairly open, but by 1885 building work had hemmed the ground in with rows of terraced houses. The expansion of housing brought with it a concurrent school-building programme, so that in the spring of 1886 Manningham's ground was compulsorily purchased to facilitate the erection of a school. With only a single summer in which to find a site and construct a new ground, Manningham's options were limited. They had to find an undeveloped and affordable location. Unlike their rivals Bradford RFC, who drew their support from all corners of the town, Manningham were forced to restrict their horizons and remain as close as possible to their core support in the Manningham district. Eventually a site was identified at the bottom of Valley Parade.

And thus was born Bradford's present-day football stadium. The then site owners, the Midland Railway Company, gave the club an initial seven-year lease. The development of Valley Parade tripled Manningham's membership and gave the club record gate receipts. In contrast to the use of public subscriptions used to develop Park

Avenue, the construction of Valley Parade was financed by loans from the club members.

Stepping back from the minutiae of rugby's evolution in Bradford and across the nation, we should not lose sight of the overridingly important outcome of the late nineteenth century's educational revolution, which was the universal adoption of a cult of athleticism. Traditionally this had always been strongly linked with schools such as Marlborough and Rugby, but it eventually arrived in many northern schools including Bramham College, Broughton College, Leeds Grammar School, St. Peter's School (York) and the Manchester schools of Broughton, Chorlton and Victoria Park.

That said, the value of encouraging physical well-being and prowess was by no means the exclusive or perhaps even the predominant ethic in the new sporting culture.

There was money to be made.

KICK-OFF

5
Profits and players: sport as a business

As the crowds, and their money, poured into rugby grounds across the north of England, a veritable army of journalists, sports promoters, sporting goods manufacturers and retailers arose to feed and profit from this sporting phenomenon. Sport was becoming a business - and one with many faces. It was expanding into all aspects of life. It was becoming a fascination and an obsession that lasted long after the referee's final whistle had blown.

In an era when amateurism and respectability were being deployed as weapons in a conflict that would ultimately split rugby asunder, sport-related businesses had the potential to raise conflicting issues for the rugby authorities. Frequently the men running businesses that profited from the popularity of sport, and in particularly rugby, were intimately connected with the hierarchy of the Rugby Football Union. Their commercial activities can hardly have passed without notice, yet while working-class players were condemned for acquiring employment in public houses or at a club patron's industrial business, the authorities remained silent about the entrepreneurial activities of middle-class players and officials.

The exponential growth of participation in the codified sports brought with it an increased demand for manufactured equipment and clothing. Given the potentially significant costs of starting such a business, it is likely that the entrepreneurs would most likely have been middle class with access to finance or someone with an existing connection to a sporting institution. One man who had a foot in both camps was Bradford's international rugby player John Joseph Hawcridge. From at least 1886 he was one of a trio of entrepreneurs who ran the British Sports Depot. From large premises in Bradford's town centre the company manufactured and sold equipment and clothing for gymnasiums, swimming, skating, curling, cricket, golf, archery, hockey, quoits, football and lawn tennis. The scale of the operation is illustrated by the fact that twenty-four employees (one fifth of the total) were dedicated to the manufacture of footballs, and their rugby balls had been selected by the RFU as the standard for size, shape and quality.

The British Sports Depot's goods were reportedly distributed to all parts of Britain and the colonies. A newspaper as far away as New Zealand reported in 1887 on an enlargement of the British Sports Depot's premises, and the comprehensive nature of the firm's catalogue. However, the following year Hawcridge agreed a division of the company and he himself departed from the British Sports Depot to concentrate on a 'hatters and hosiers' shop. Hawcridge's brother, William, continued trading as an 'athletic outfitter' and was based at the 'Skating Rink, Valley Parade' (adjacent to Manningham RFC's ground) until his company was declared bankrupt in 1890. JJ Hawcridge's hat business was voluntarily wound up in 1893, and the famous England international died in San Francisco in 1905 aged only forty-two.

There was certainly money to be made from sport's own industrial revolution. For those who took up directorships with clubs, or organisational roles within sporting bodies, taking direct profits was usually debarred. However, many did profit indirectly, and perhaps one man who epitomised this was Tony Fattorini. Probably the best known of the Bradford companies that diversified into sporting goods was his jewellery firm. Descended from Italian immigrants, it was after the arrival in Bradford of Tony Fattorini in 1882 that the trade in sporting trophies was greatly increased. His interest in rugby probably stemmed from his schooling in Harrogate where he played rugby under the supervision of Teddy Bartram, the famous Wakefield goal-kicker and later the first player to be charged with professionalism by the Rugby Football Union. Fattorini was later a member of Manningham RFC and enjoyed a long association with the Valley Parade club that lasted into the twentieth century and the emergence of Bradford City AFC.

Fattorini's jewellery business began designing and producing gold and silver medals for schools and colleges, cups and medals for sporting clubs, awards for flower shows, chess clubs, learned societies and hundreds of other organisations throughout the country.

Fattorini's fortune was inextricably tied to sport. In later years he would represent Manningham at the meeting when the Rugby League was formed; become a director of Bradford City AFC, the elected president of six cross-country athletic associations, and vice-president of the Amateur Athletics Association; and be appointed as timekeeper for the King's Cup air race around Britain, for four Olympic Games (Paris, London, Stockholm, Amsterdam), and for the event where Malcolm Campbell set an unofficial world speed record driving his famous Blue Bird.

In 1907 Fattorini's formed a subsidiary company entitled Sports & Pastimes, which manufactured and sold sporting clothing and equipment. Their clients included Bradford City AFC, who wore shirts supplied by Sports & Pastimes when they won the FA Cup in 1911. Remarkably, the 1911 FA Cup competition saw the first use of the current trophy, which was designed by Fattorini's. That, alongside the production of the Rugby League Challenge Cup, is Fattorini's greatest sporting legacy.

The commercial opportunities offered by large attendances at rugby matches, and the growing fame of the players, were also exploited by people who did not have a direct involvement in the game. One such man was John Baines, whose company was founded almost adjacent to Manningham's Carlisle Road ground in 1885. In that year Baines invented and patented football collectors' cards. Over the following century the collecting of football cards became a global obsession. The fact that it had its roots in Victorian Bradford is further evidence of the sophistication and popularity of the town's rugby culture in the 1880s and 1890s.

Baines' cards were a manifestation of a new celebrity culture. While the feting of rugby players probably marked a welcome rise in the status and esteem of working-class sportsmen, what Baines represents is arguably a large-scale commercial exploitation of this celebrity culture. Packets of six cards were sold for a ha'penny, which was often the entire pocket-money of a Bradford boy during that era. Rugby players and their clubs were the staple product, though the range of cards was expanded to cover cricket and football.

The card craze spread through the land and through all classes. Cards illustrating players and teams from south Wales, Scotland, the English midlands and the north were produced, the latter making up by far the largest proportion of surviving cards. This probably reflects the fact that the north of England was the most advanced area as regards the commercialisation of rugby, and that it lay within easy reach of Baines' manufacturing base. The societal expansion of the cards' subjects is arguably the best evidence of rugby's popularity among an increasing proportion of the population. Schools teams, church clubs and even works teams are featured on Baines' cards.

John Baines and fellow Bradford manufacturer W.N. Sharpe dominated the football card market until the 1920s. Bradford's printing industry had undergone a rapid expansion during the nineteenth century. In 1820 the town had four printing works; by 1900 seventy were in operation. The production of football cards in Bradford was connected to the advanced state of the printing trade in the town, which was probably the result of commercial and cultural links with Germany that would have given early access to continental printing, and in particular lithographical developments. The commercial advantage this gave Bradford facilitated the large-scale production of football cards.

The grip rugby had on the imagination of Bradford's male population was reflected in the finances of the town's two main rugby clubs. And it was not just the male population. A report regarding an 1884 match - Manningham's opening game of the season against Hull - offers a rare and tantalising statistic: of the five thousand strong crowd, around one quarter were women. How representative was this of a typical match?

In the early days women were admitted for free. Did this subtly convey a sense of 'appendage' status, rather than women being taken seriously as committed supporters? Since they weren't contributing to the clubs' finances, would this have affected whether, for example, toilets were provided for female spectators?

In fact much greater attendances than this, going into five figures, were now a regular feature. Examples include a crowd of sixteen thousand witnessing a North versus South representative fixture at Park Avenue in 1885, ten thousand at Bradford's opening game of the 1886-7 season against Halifax, and thirteen thousand at an 1886 Yorkshire Cup tie between Bradford and Manningham. Even if a quarter of those crowds were non-paying females, clubs were making healthy profits.

But canny clubs were eyeing their gate takings, and thus it was, with competition between clubs intensifying, that charges were introduced for women. As early as 1885 - possibly being the first club to do this - Preston North End (in the Football League) introduced charges, having noted the attendance of a grand army of two thousand women at a particular match.

Charges for women must inevitably have played a role in the considerable decline, by the end of the century, of women's spectatorship. By the 1890s, reports of the presence of any women spectators became rare. The women typically managed the household budget, and may have seen this payment for a purely recreational activity as an indulgence, when there were mouths to feed, and an easy saving to make. The charges, coupled with the endemic use of foul language in the largely male throng, may have clinched women's decision to forego a Saturday afternoon of sports.

The participation of women as players of rugby or football in that era was nigh on unthinkable. As said in an earlier chapter, the story of women in spectator sports in Bradford does not substantially begin until the twentieth century, which is beyond the remit of this publication. While there were some rare instances of women's teams if one looks nationwide (it is thought that the first recorded game of women's football was in 1888 in Inverness, Scotland), it would not be until 1917 that the first recorded women's football teams were active in Bradford.

The Football Association's 1921 ban on women playing sports at Football League grounds was a massive blow, having long-term ramifications. The FA's attitude speaks volumes about the absolute sidelining of women's sports in popular culture which was, and some might say, is to this day, governed by men both on the field and in the commercial sphere. Further, the fact that this ban was not lifted until 1971 reflects poorly on, and asks uncomfortable questions of, the so-called 'people's game'. Until the revival of women's football in the 1980s, the game in Bradford was hence limited for most of the twentieth century to one-off events.

Back to the 1880s, and Manningham was rising and rising in popularity and hence profitability. This is demonstrated by comparing receipts taken at the gate. After the first season at Park

Avenue, 1880-1, Bradford RFC's receipts were £520; by the 1885-6 season they had risen to £3,120. By contrast, Manningham's receipts for the 1886-7 season were £1,907. However, as the Bradford Observer noted, the figures quoted were almost certainly some way short of what was actually taken at the gate. 'The trick can be done by manipulating the gate money before it becomes a cash book item'. As success attracted higher crowds and improved receipts, the undeclared money was almost certainly used to pay players and thereby attract the best talent.

Partly in response to the Football Association's (FA) legalisation of professionalism in 1885, in October 1886 the Rugby Football Union's Annual General Meeting passed new rules aimed at eliminating creeping professionalism in the oval ball game. Payment was debarred for services rendered, compensation for loss of wages, training, transfer fees or promise of employment, and monies in excess of hotel or travelling expenses. Bradford's Harry Garnett, the voice of a significant minority in Yorkshire opposed to professionalism, declared 'if working men desired to play football, they should pay for it themselves, as they would have to do for any other pleasure'. However, for middle class players the rules were less rigorous and they were able to receive generous 'gifts' without censure.

Less than a week prior to the adoption of the new rules, Bradford's captain and England international half-back, Fred Bonsor, had been presented with a gold watch worth twenty guineas and a purse containing £80. The gifts were described as a testimonial and wedding present. The largesse shown towards Bonsor could have hardly avoided the gaze of the RFU as it was presented following a match against Liverpool, which nine thousand people attended and which was refereed by the Rev. Frank Marshall, president of the YRU and a man who has been described as the 'scourge of professionalism'. Similarly a few months earlier Bradford's committee had given their England forward Laurie Hickson a wedding present comprising 'a clock and ornaments'.

Corruption was coming to characterise the rugby scene. The 1886 Yorkshire Cup brought with it allegations that Manningham was attracting playing talent from around the region by offering payments 'over and above expenses'. In what many believed was pre-planned action, Manningham became the first club to be charged with 'professionalism'. Pudsey lodged an appeal following their first round defeat, alleging that Manningham had paid Jack Birmingham and William Pulleyn. Both were natives of Selby and a witness said they had 'received broken-time payments, rail-fare and a sovereign'. Manningham's captain Billy Fawcett admitted that the club had promised to find Pulleyn a job in Bradford, but denied the other charges. Pulleyn had been a joinery apprentice and his former employer alleged that he had held up a postal order and said 'who will work here when he gets paid for football?' He had been frequently absent and had boasted to work mates that the postal orders had been sent by Manningham. Birmingham had been invited to play for Manningham when he 'accidentally' met Billy Fawcett in Selby. Quite what the Manningham captain was doing wandering the streets of Selby fully thirty miles from Bradford was not explained.

In the event, the YRU committee rejected Pudsey's appeal on the grounds that the evidence failed to prove that anything more than the 'third class rail fare' had been paid to the players.

The gate money being generated by the rugby clubs were reflective of the increasing crowds attending rugby matches in Yorkshire. Accommodating those crowds in fairly rudimentary grounds was both a logistical challenge and a financial opportunity. Of course, once it was obvious that spectators were willing to pay to watch a match, the prevention of others from watching without payment was the starting point of enclosed grounds. Initially large canvas screens were erected around the perimeters. In time, high wooden fences replaced the screens, and the grounds became enclosed facilities for which spectators could be charged gate money. Prior to the adoption of turnstiles the collection of money from spectators was the responsibility of club officials walking around the ground with wooden collection boxes.

As crowds grew into the thousands, the problem of giving the spectators a view of the pitch had to be solved. Apart from small, usually uncovered 'grandstands' comprising wooden benches, the vast majority of spectators were packed onto poorly constructed embankments. Early terraces were sloping banks constructed from ash, cinders and even rubbish. As there were few parallels to draw on, and little or no official regulation, the spectator boom was almost bound to lead to incidents large and small.

Arguably, Manningham RFC was one of the most vulnerable clubs, given that they had been forced to construct the eighteen-thousand-capacity Valley Parade ground over the course of a single summer. The move tripled the club's membership and increased crowds to record levels. But on Christmas Day 1888, the ground's shortcomings were exposed. There was only one central entrance into the Midland Road side and, with a crowd of sixteen thousand inside, there was congestion around the halfway line. A number of boys had been passed over the heads of the spectators to be placed in front of the pitch-side barrier. Seven minutes into the game there was a surge forward as people strained to watch the action and the barrier collapsed, trapping the boys beneath it.

The referee halted the game as players and spectators rushed to extract four boys from the melee. Twelve year-old Thomas Coyle was pronounced dead as a result of a broken neck. Three other boys suffered injuries, the worst of which was a broken right thigh. The game was abandoned once word of the fatality spread. The officials agreed that the gate receipts of £115 should be donated to the dead boy's relatives.

Three days later, on 28 December 1888, an inquest was held at Bradford Town Hall where evidence was given in front of a jury. William Jackson had helped move several boys from in front of the fencing before the game kicked off. He was in charge of the spare ball and had just returned the ball to the players when he heard the fence give way behind him. The fallen railings were lifted clear and the boys extracted. Thomas Coyle was sitting in a doubled up position, but appeared to be dead. Jackson said he had seen the railings put up when the ground was constructed two years previously. They were made from new wood and went into the ground to a depth of around two feet. Another witness, James Riley, a boot maker, of Manningham, said he had seen several lads come from the boys' enclosure into the Midland Road. Though club officials sent most back to the boys' enclosure, those who had escaped into the crowd were eventually passed to the front. He said the crowd became packed in the middle part of the banking because it gave the best view. He saw a ten-yard section of fencing collapse and then the portion directly in front of him gave way. It fell onto the lads and he found himself in a heap of bodies. A twenty-yard section of fencing adjoining the fatal portion had fallen the previous season, albeit without injury. Bradford's Chief Constable said it was possible that the two year-old ground, which had extensive ash bankings, had yet to properly settle.

The borough surveyor reported that a twenty-yard portion had collapsed exactly opposite the Midland Road entrance. The wood of the posts was in remarkably good order. He remarked that the forces that caused it to collapse must have been 'considerable'.

So the jury recommended that the central entrance be closed, and two opened at either end of the Midland Road enclosure. Parallel barriers (similar to contemporary crush barriers) were also recommended. A verdict of 'accidental death' was returned. Thomas Coyle was buried at Undercliffe Cemetery, and Manningham RFC paid the funeral expenses.

The crush that resulted in the fatality at Valley Parade appears to have been far from unique. A perimeter fence collapse at Park Avenue in 1898 resulted in hundreds of people falling onto the pitch, fortunately without serious injury. Such incidents were becoming commonplace, with a whole run occurring in quick succession in the following eight years during matches at Park Avenue in 1899 and 1904, Batley in 1902, Hunslet in 1903, and Keighley in 1905.

The death of Thomas Coyle at Valley Parade thus proved to be only the first of many in over a century. What is notable is that the underlying causes, such as congestion near the central entrance and the surge of spectators at an exciting moment in the match, are familiar to modern football spectators. Of course, in the modern era the capacity of grounds is known and measured, whereas in the Victorian and Edwardian eras, ground capacities and attendances were estimates. Club officials probably learned how to manage crowds by trial and error. As crowds continued to grow, the facilities offered by clubs struggled to keep up with the demand. The surprise is only that there were not many more such pitch invasions and resulting serious incidents.

The large crowds passing through the turnstiles of the Yorkshire rugby clubs gave those organisations an economic advantage and commercial imperative to attract the best playing talent. However, it was not simply a zero-sum game. The highly competitive rugby being played in Yorkshire, the white rose county, produced skilled players and tacticians. Thus it was perhaps no surprise when the prophecy at last came to pass. Thirteen years after the Yorkshire Cup was founded with the stated aim 'Yorkshire shall be able to play the rest of England and beat it', the national side was defeated in 1890 by a Yorkshire XV at Park Avenue.

Victory! And a demonstration of Yorkshire rugby's awesomely rapid achievement of power and economic might. The players received specially struck medals. Yorkshire's triumph was rewarded with seven white rose players being selected to represent England against Scotland at Edinburgh the following Saturday. The Yorkshiremen helped England to victory, thereby justifying their inclusion in the national XV.

Despite the tensions in the game, the shared national triumph was an opportunity to heal the rift between north and south. Since the then president of the English Rugby Union was Bradford's Harry Garnett, 1890 was potentially going to be a defining year.

The year indeed proved a historic one for the game, but the underlying theme was exclusivity, not inclusivity.

The previous decade had seen rugby evolve from being a middle-class social recreation into a game increasingly dominated by working-class participation and spectators. Of course, the commercialisation of rugby could not have occurred without substantial entrepreneurial involvement. It is important to remember the central role played by middle-class entrepreneurs who facilitated the influx of working-class players and spectators into the game.

The tensions that beset rugby in the 1890s have often been framed as a class war. To the classically educated gentlemen of England, defeat by a Yorkshire team of mainly working-class players was viewed as an affront to the natural order. As was written in the classic Greek Iliad of their schooldays, 'the main function of the ordinary folk was to be killed by their superiors: it is unthinkable for a hero to be slain except by another hero' (from Richard Jenkyns' book 'The Victorians and Ancient Greece').

But in many respects this was an intra-class conflict; at its heart the replacement of an ethical elite by a business one. The entrepreneurs, usually from a capitalist industrial background, shared in the main the culture of the working class that viewed sport as a form of entertainment rather than a moral force. Indeed, the emergence of professionalism in sport was a product of the wave of commercialism which engulfed the leisure sector in the late nineteenth century.

Less than eight weeks after Yorkshire's vanquishing of England, the Southern Nomads played in Bradford. The touring team was selected largely from the Blackheath club. In the late evening of 7th April 1890, William Carpmael was enjoying an oyster supper at Leuchters' Restaurant on Darley Street in central Bradford. He conceived the idea of a selected touring team with no members and no home ground. They would be known as the Barbarians. Carpmael retired to the Alexandra Hotel to further discuss the idea, and at two o'clock in the morning, the Barbarians was formed.

A team selected by invitation, and which chose its opponents, was effectively a rejection of the rising tide of working-class participation in 1890s rugby. Although the Barbarians was reputedly open to 'gentlemen of all classes', a mere handful of northern players were invited to join the team on tour. The under-representation of northern players in the ranks of the Barbarians probably reflected the club's selection policy, but a factor that should not be discounted is that most northern players were simply unavailable due to their host clubs' busy fixture schedules.

For only two years did the Barbarians bother with the north, regularly playing Bradford, Huddersfield, Hartlepool and Swinton between 1890 and 1892. The year after that they abandoned the vast majority of their northern fixtures in favour of matches in the south-west and south Wales.

And so it was that Bradford had neither sight nor sound of the Barbarians for more than seventy years, until, in 1965, they finally re-met Bradford RUFC at Lidget Green as part of their seventy-fifth season tour.

6
The coming of the rugby and football leagues

Britain was nearing the end of the industrial boom-century, and both on and off the field of play the working classes were asserting their rights. Sport and society were steadily becoming more democratic. The Manningham Mills strike (1890-1) led to an event that would irrevocably change the face of British politics: the formation of the Independent Labour Party.

In sport, the development of league systems introduced a structure and rhythm that remains in place to this day. It was a transformational moment every bit as significant as the changes being wrought in the political arena.

In local and national politics, the 1890s saw liberalism's popular support undermined by rising trade union membership, which in Bradford rose from three and a half thousand in 1883 to almost four times that number less than a decade later (1892). The Manningham Mills strike, a five-month dispute (December 1890 to April 1891) triggered by a reduction in wages at Lister & Company's mill, proved to be a watershed moment. The strike turned into a free speech issue after the authorities attempted to prevent rallies in the town centre.

Did the Manningham strike, and the belt-tightening among families due to the loss of wages, affect attendances of the Saturday game? Manningham's gate takings for that period did not show any reduction. Male leisure spending appears to have been insulated from the undoubted financial pressures caused by the dispute, revealing something of the relationship of husband and wife as regards responsibilities for thrift. Manningham even played fund-raising matches to aid the strikers, which raises an interesting contradiction that some of those in attendance may have been both donators to and recipients of the strike fund. Did the women ever exhort their men to stay home and save?

The dispute culminated in high drama. On the night of 23rd April 1891, the workers rioted, and the riot was put down by the Durham Light Infantry. The strike collapsed soon after. However, the strike had eroded the deferential attitude of the working class to politics. The result was momentous: the formation of the Independent Labour Party (ILP).

From 1891 onwards, Manningham consistently returned ILP councillors. By 1906 only a Liberal-Conservative pact prevented the ILP from holding the balance of power on the city council. The ILP was not just a political party, it became an ethical, cultural and social movement. It has even been claimed that the ILP replaced, to some extent, the role of the church in the life of some families. As regards sports in this sphere, there was a Labour Cricket League, but the ILP appears to have remained largely aloof from popular sporting culture. This probably reflects a general unease in the Socialist movement towards sport. Social historian Susan Barton suggests that some socialists *saw entrepreneurs' manipulation of workers' leisure activities as a threat to developing an independent class-consciousness.*

In parallel to the political turmoil, the textile trade suffered a setback with the imposition of the McKinley tariff (1891) which halved trade with America. Although the easing of tariffs in the mid-1890s led to a short-lived upsurge in production, it was rapidly reversed by the introduction of the Dingley tariff in 1898, which reduced trade to its lowest level since the early part of the century. The tariffs saw manufacturers looking to the new markets of the British Empire.

By 1897 exports to the Empire made up practically a third of Bradford's output. Despite the opening of new markets, the tariffs pushed Bradford down the production cycle. To aid their textile industries, countries placed low import duties on goods that could be exploited by their manufacturers. As a result, exports of tops (combed wool prepared for spinning) and noils (short pieces produced during combing) rose by forty percent between 1890 and 1901. In contrast, piece goods increased by only four percent. The numbers of unskilled and semi-skilled workers employed in Bradford's mills rose accordingly. The overseas competition heralded a reduction in profits and a downward pressure on wages as manufacturers sought to reduce overheads. Piece rates and increased machinery speeds became common. The eventual easing of tariffs saw four millions pounds' worth of goods exported to America in 1909. The following year the city exported forty-two million pounds' worth of goods to overseas markets.

	1801	1911	Rate of population increase
Essen	4 000	295 000	7 275%
Bradford	8 000	288 000	3 500%
Dusseldorf	10 000	359 000	3 490%
Leipzig	30 000	590 000	1 867%
Hanover	18 000	302 000	1 578%
Budapest	54 000	880 000	1 530%
Stuttgart	18 000	286 000	1 489%
Sheffield	31 000	465 000	1 400%
Munich	40 000	596 000	1 390%
Glasgow	77 000	1 000 000	1 199%

Throughout the peaks and troughs of the textile trade, Bradford's population continued to expand. In the three decades from 1851 it grew by 86.5%, and in the subsequent three decades (until 1911) a further 48.4%. Bradford's percentage growth in the space of a hundred and ten years (1801- 1911) was the second highest of Europe's forty-eight largest cities, topped only by Essen in Germany. Notably, where British cities dominate the growth figures in the period 1801 to 1851, it is their German industrial counterparts that had the greatest population expansion between 1851 and 1911. Budapest is the sole non-British or German city in the top ten.

Commercialised spectator sport was by now on track for becoming the big business it is today. Bradford's growing population was widening and deepening the market. The massive popularity of rugby's Yorkshire Cup meant that by the 1890s it had begun to overshadow the ordinary matches, which were in danger of being viewed as little more than glorified practice matches.

Yet despite the keen interest in gate takings, the potential market of women supporters seems to have been disregarded, even though women were now, unlike in rugby's early days, charged admission and could well have brought clubs significant additional income. The fact is that attitudes towards women among the rugby hierarchy became increasingly dismissive as a 'culture of manliness' took hold.

Rugby clubs started to make big, risky decisions. Their constructions of large-capacity grounds for cup-ties in order to attract, and probably recompense, the best playing talent, locked them into a cycle of financial uncertainty. An early exit from the cup could potentially be ruinous. Clearly the clubs now required something more than a fixture-list of friendly or 'ordinary' games, as the press described them, whose attractiveness was declining in the face of the raw excitement of the cup-ties.

Football had already faced a similar quandary in the wake of the adoption of open professionalism five years earlier. The solution was the brainchild of Aston Villa's William McGregor: a Football League, established in 1888, with a fixed schedule of home and away matches. The league was an immediate success with clubs, enjoying increased gate receipts almost across the board.

And so to rugby's first league. The Football League provided a readymade template for rugby to follow. Thus, four years later, during the summer of 1892, an alliance of the top 'gate taking' clubs of Yorkshire rugby tabled a proposal for a self-governing league, entitled the Yorkshire Senior Competition (YSC). The word 'league' was not used in the title of the new organisation, as the Yorkshire Rugby Union (YRU) felt it was too closely related to professionalism.

However, the Yorkshire Rugby Union committee, fearful of having its authority usurped by a cartel of the top clubs, refused to sanction the Yorkshire Senior Competition, and made a counter proposal of a league involving every Yorkshire team. The YSC clubs threatened to withdraw from the Yorkshire Cup unless their own proposed league was accepted. This threat to the integrity of the cup was too much for the YRU, so in late August they conceded to the YSC's threat, and voted unanimously to accept their league.

Although the Yorkshire Senior Competition clubs had clearly won, the Yorkshire Rugby Union managed to insert a clause into the agreement that it reserved the right to override any decisions made by the YSC clubs. However, the YSC was effectively a separate body and still had wide-ranging powers, which included 'all questions of qualification, match schedules, disputes and player transfers'.

The formation of the Yorkshire Senior Competition illustrated the fact that the balance of power was beginning to shift towards the clubs. It also set in train, or at least significantly accelerated, a series of events that would shape rugby's future for the following century. The Pall Mall Gazette stated the obvious when it said that the leading Yorkshire clubs were 'slowly but surely' moving away from amateurism. It thought that the league format would attract ever-larger crowds and 'with so much money, professionalism is inevitable'.

The formalised fixture list of the Yorkshire Senior Competition brought regular and lucrative meetings with local rivals. With meaning now added to the non-cup matches, five-figure crowds could be attracted to the best YSC fixtures. In particular, derby matches became highly anticipated fixtures.

Both Bradford and Manningham had particularly strong sides when the YSC was formed. An intense rivalry was forming between the two clubs, and this was reflected in the attendances the matches attracted. At Park Avenue on Boxing Day 1893 a 'derby' crowd of eighteen and a half thousand generated record gate receipts of four hundred and sixteen pounds and nine shillings. It was a level of popularity that arguably only the Football League could match.

Bradford's two derby victories over Manningham during 1892-3 must have been especially satisfying, as they helped them to win the inaugural Yorkshire Senior Competition championship shield. At Bradford's Annual General Meeting it was asserted that if Bradford were to retain its prominence in the game, they would 'have to increase their accommodation' and thus, they hoped, their gate receipts.

Of course, expanding the ground would incur substantial capital expenditure. This was complicated by the fact that the football club shared its profits with its parent: Bradford Cricket Athletic & Football Club (BCA&FC). As the rugby club's income increased, it was perhaps natural that a re-evaluation of the relationships between the constituent bodies would occur. Those tensions seem to have been apparent, as one official complained that during his time on the rugby club's committee they had handed over £15,000 to the BCA&FC, adding that it was time that the rugby section 'spent a little more on themselves'.

The tensions evident at Park Avenue would only have been heightened when, in the following season, Manningham not only defeated Bradford in the two derby matches, but also won the 1893-4 YSC championship. When the Manningham team arrived at

Bradford Exchange station they were met by a reported ten thousand well-wishers. The Manningham Brass Band played 'See the conquering hero come'. Manningham Lane was 'thronged with promenading football enthusiasts' as a celebration dinner took place at the Belle Vue. The league format had managed to widen the popular appeal of rugby beyond the cup competitions. It marked the emergence of a recognisably modern sporting culture and landscape. There was a defined season with its rhythm of league matches punctuated by cup-ties. The local newspapers carried pen pictures of players that began to evolve into interviews.

One player who attracted the attention of the media was Manningham's New Zealander, George Stephenson. He introduced an element of internationalism, or at least the wider British Empire, into the domestic Rugby Union game. His arrival in Bradford in 1891 coincided with the previously mentioned realignment of the Bradford textile trade towards the markets of the Empire in the wake of the imposition of American trade tariffs.

In some respects it could be said that Stephenson was a physical representation of those changes, as Stephenson's father, a wool merchant, had arranged for his son to expand his knowledge of the trade with Reddiough & Son. Even prior to the American trade tariffs, Bradford had well-established trading links with Australia and New Zealand: as early as 1800, one hundred thousand pounds (in imperial weight) of wool had been imported for use in Bradford's mills. By 1874, with British wool in short supply, a staggering 225,462,101 pounds of wool arrived from the antipodes. The importance of this market is illustrated by the fact that Bradford manufacturers established wool-purchasing offices in Adelaide, Melbourne and Sydney.

Despite this lucrative trade, the nineteen-year-old Stephenson appears to have treated his time in the wool capital of the world as something of an extended holiday, with playing rugby the number one priority. During his time at Valley Parade he scored twenty-one tries in forty games and helped his club become champions of the Yorkshire Senior Competition. However, Stephenson's father was not impressed by his son's success on the field of play, and recalled him to New Zealand during the summer of 1894.

It is impossible to know definitively whether Stephenson was paid during his spell with Manningham, but given the prevailing climate it is probable he received some kind of recompense. In 1893, northern clubs had attempted to have broken-time payments to players made legal. This was far from full-blown professionalism, being framed purely as compensation for players who would lose money when absent from work when playing for their clubs. However, it was rejected at the Rugby Football Union's 1893 Annual General Meeting.

In the wake of this attempt to legalise a form of, albeit compensatory, payment, the Rugby Football Union significantly hardened its stance on 'professionalism' allegations, thus Huddersfield, Leigh, Salford and Wigan were subsequently suspended. The plight of the suspended clubs and banned players attracted widespread sympathy in the northern media. One interesting case was the former Manningham captain Billy Fawcett, who was banned for life by the RFU. Fawcett had been captain for the three years to 1888, and so when he emigrated to Canada in 1890 to become a cattle farmer, his pals at Valley Parade gave him a £29 leaving present - to buy a piano. However, when he returned to Bradford four years later (to become the licensee of the Peel Hotel), the gift classed him as a professional in the eyes of the RFU.

As professionalism rules were tightened, clubs and individuals sought ways of circumventing them. A favourite ruse was to install players as landlords in public houses close to their home grounds. The brewers were delighted with the increase in trade a popular footballer would bring, while the player, in all probability completely ignorant of the licensing trade, welcomed the wages and freedom to train and play in mid-week matches. Indeed, Yorkshire Owl informed its readers they could spend a 'football evening' in Bradford, listing eleven pubs in the centre that were run by, or connected with, players of Bradford and Manningham.

Sports networks were now spreading transnationally – as was the standing of Manningham RFC in the game of rugby. Hence the invitation that came in December 1894 for Manningham to play Stade Français. There is no doubt that the French were fully aware of the 'formidable reputation' of Manningham. As The Graphic wrote, *hitherto, French footballers have been satisfied with pitting themselves against our third or fourth-class teams; but no doubt they have heard of the fame of the Yorkshire football and long to see some of it.*

Manningham thus became only the fourth English club to play in Europe (following the Civil Service, Oxford University and Rosslyn Park clubs). That a match in Paris was viable is one illustration of the transformation of communications, transport and associational connections that was evolving constantly through the two decades preceding the turn of the century and the two decades after it. This was sport becoming international.

While the prowess of Manningham on the field of play is the likely reason for their appearance on the playing fields of Paris, there is the possibility that trading links could have played a part. France was both a competitor and important market for Bradford's textile trade. Undoubtedly that will have resulted in the formation of commercial and social links. The early rugby tours facilitated the building of social networks, illustrated by the fact that Sir John Astley and Lord Dufferin, both of whom were present at early Anglo-French rugby matches, met Pierre de Coubertin at those matches and subsequently joined him on the first Olympic committee. And of course, among Manningham's official party was that great entrepreneur, Tony Fattorini. He had strong links with athletics, but how did he get to be a timekeeper at several Olympic games - and a member of the International Olympic Committee? It is very likely that Fattorini encountered Pierre de Coubertin at the Paris game against Manningham, and that this resulted in Fattorini's involvement with the Olympic movement.

What is perhaps surprising about Manningham's trip to Paris was the amount of supporters who travelled with the team. As tickets were priced at three pounds, eighteen shillings and sixpence, around three times higher than the average weekly wage, it is likely that the travellers would have come from the middle class. A special train was arranged, complete with Pullman dining and parlour cars and ordinary saloon carriages.

On the afternoon of Saturday 1st December 1894, a large crowd of supporters gathered to see the party of one hundred and thirty-five folk depart for the French capital. Around seventy supporters travelled with the players and officials. They arrived in Paris at 5.38 the following morning. After resting at a hotel, Manningham met Stade Français at Vélodrome de Courbevoie. A crowd of around fifteen hundred witnessed an easy 27-0 victory for Manningham. The following day the party visited Versailles and on the Tuesday viewed the principal sites of Paris. Meanwhile back home there were more than raised eyebrows about the trip, with accusations of payments having been made to players. The Leeds Mercury took the side of the team: *Is it heinous [...] for the Manningham committee to pay the expenses of their team to Paris for a few days, when it is quite legitimate for a crack southern team to tour for a week at the expense of the clubs they play?*

As the majority of Manningham's players were drawn from the working classes, it was perhaps inevitable that their trip to France would set off such a discussion.

More controversy...

7
The rise and decline of rugby's Northern Union

The 'Great Split' of rugby into what we know today as the Rugby League and Rugby Union is rightly viewed as one of the defining moments of sporting history. Rugby's civil war has often been described as a working-class revolt, but the main actors were the solidly middle-class leaders of northern rugby who had gained their wealth from industrial capitalism.

Northern rugby had developed into a highly competitive and commercialised spectator sport. Sport was becoming ever more democratic. Rugby was arguably the last middle-class bastion of recreational leisure in the context of team sport. A decade earlier football, and to a lesser extent cricket, had made compromises, conceding to rising working-class involvement, but in the context of 1890s Britain with rising trade union membership and the emergence of the Independent Labour Party, the rugby authorities were in no mood for concessions.

Suspensions of clubs, bans handed down to players, accusations of hidden payments levelled against Manningham in the wake of their Paris trip... Tensions within the game of rugby were coming to a head. Things finally boiled over when in 1894, the Rugby Football Union introduced a highly controversial motion. It stated that any club or player charged with professionalism would be considered guilty until they proved otherwise. Whether it was a move to bolster the tenets of amateurism, or deliberate provocation designed to cause a rupture of the game on a north-south axis, is debatable. Whatever, it was widely viewed as an affront to natural justice and 'un-English'. Due to huge opposition, the RFU withdrew the motion.

However, only a few months later the Rugby Football Union was reported to be considering a proposal to abolish all leagues. The leading clubs of Lancashire and Yorkshire immediately discussed the formation of a Northern Union as a mutual protection society, with transfers between clubs regulated and an annual challenge match arranged between the champions of Lancashire and Yorkshire. However, an initially secret clause stating that in the event of a member-club being expelled or punished by the RFU, the club would have the right to appeal to the Northern Union, indicated a degree of autonomy that was a direct challenge to the hegemony of the RFU. Apparently in favour of ongoing national rugby unity, Bradford, Huddersfield and Leeds at this point declined to be 'a party to any movement which would entail expulsion from the ranks of the Rugby Union'.

But in August 1895 tensions were ratcheted up again when the Rugby Football Union withdrew the powers given to the Yorkshire Seniors Competition clubs, quoting their existing rule that 'any independent league or combination is expressly forbidden'. This made organising the season's fixtures impossible and, combined with the expulsion of the YSC clubs from the Yorkshire Cup, it left the clubs in a very difficult position.

Solutions had to be found. Bradford, Halifax, Huddersfield and Leeds planned to field strictly amateur teams for the coming season, a move that was described by an unnamed official as 'unconditional surrender' to the RFU. It was thought that Bradford, Huddersfield and Leeds would subsidise their amateur teams (and presumably the loss of fixtures against virtually all their Yorkshire rivals) by means of 'rather extensively' adopting association football. This would have served as a kind of insurance policy: in the event of being banned by the RFU, the clubs would have soccer to fall back on. Another motive might have been that a professional or semi-professional association football team could subsidise amateur rugby union, providing the income required to repay the substantial outlay already expended on the grounds at Park Avenue, Fartown and Headingley.

Meanwhile, the rest of the Yorkshire Seniors Competition clubs, including Manningham, announced they would form a new union 'with or without ... Bradford, Huddersfield and Leeds'. The three dissenting clubs were still intent on continued allegiance to the Rugby Football Union with its national rather than regional remit, thus Bradford's Harry Briggs went down to London to meet Rowland Hill of the RFU. Briggs handed Hill a series of questions, including: 'What support could Bradford, Leeds and Huddersfield obtain from southern clubs if they rejoined the Yorkshire Union'? Hill's letter of reply informed the clubs that even if they remained within the union, they could not expect to be allocated games against the top southern clubs.

Rugby's historic rupture was thus inevitable. Effectively cut adrift by the Rugby Football Union, and economically bound by large mortgages on their expensively developed grounds, Bradford, Huddersfield and Leeds were left with no alternative but to join the Northern Union.

Because the Northern Union was the birth-child of rugby's split, it is tempting to frame the dispute as a north-south divide. However, it is important to remember that the Yorkshire Rugby Union was a central actor in the split. Some of amateurism's strongest adherents were Yorkshiremen: Harry Garnett of Bradford; the Rev. Frank Marshall of Huddersfield; and James Miller of Leeds. It is noteworthy that the big trio of Bradford, Huddersfield and Leeds were partly represented by those men, and this begs the question as to why a compromise could not have been negotiated.

The answer probably lies with the commercialism and competitiveness of industrial capitalism. Of the trio, only Garnett was an industrialist, but he had been educated at Blackheath

Preparatory School and his brothers had attended Rugby School. By contrast, the majority of the committee men, players and supporters of the leading clubs would have been all too familiar with the daily reality of a business seeking to gain a commercial advantage, or the worker labouring to put a meal on the family table. When viewed in that context, perhaps the Rugby Football Union was correct to conclude that compromise in 1895 would have only delayed the inevitable confrontation. For amateurism to survive in a capitalist society it had to cut adrift those elements who were unwilling, or unable, to accept and defer to its tenets.

That said, when further challenges to amateurism arose in places such as the east Midlands and south Wales, a blind eye had to be turned in order to keep Rugby Union credible as a national sport. Perhaps the overriding factor was the social tensions of the 1890s. When football resolved its issues with professionalism in the 1880s, it was against a backdrop of relative prosperity. By contrast, the 1890s was a decade of strikes and social unrest. Additionally, the adherents of amateurism had no other codified team sport to retreat to. Rugby could be viewed as amateurism's last bastion in the context of team sports. A huge amount of emotion and identity had been invested in the game, and by 1895 it probably represented much more than a mere pastime.

The momentous event of the Northern Union's formation took place on 29 August 1895, when representatives of twenty-one clubs met at Huddersfield. Twenty resigned from the Rugby Football Union and signed up for the new body. The decision to form the Northern Union was ratified almost unanimously at club meetings. There were 100% votes in favour at Broughton Rangers, Hunslet, Hull, Leigh, Manningham and St Helens. Only at Bradford was there serious opposition. Three committee members and four senior players resigned in protest.

However, even at clubs where there had been unanimous backing for the Northern Union, hopes were expressed that the schism with the RFU was a temporary aberration. Manningham's Tony Fattorini wrote in the Yorkshire Post: *If the new union were properly conducted, the Rugby Union would have to recognise professionalism in some form or another in the future or they would find ere long the only support they received would be from the universities and the public schools.*

Given the entrenched attitude of the Rugby Football Union, Fattorini's hopes were forlorn, if not also a little naive. Just two years later, the RFU was to ignore professionalism within the Welsh game in order to avoid another split that could have seen Welsh clubs joining the Northern Union and potentially changing the entire dynamic of the rugby game. At this moment the likes of Fattorini must have realised that there would be no *rapprochement*. Indeed, the central core of Yorkshire Rugby Union leadership had implemented a strategy of reconstructing the YRU on the public school ethos of the 1860s and 1870s. The officials and players who remained loyal to the RFU formed a new wave of clubs. One became known as the Bradford Wanderers - an apt name given that they had no permanent home ground (a policy perhaps rooted in fundamentalist amateurism, a defiant reaction to the forces of professionalism) until they eventually settled as Bradford RUFC at Lidget Green in 1919.

Once the Northern Union had safely negotiated its first season, the practical and financial attraction of the new code resulted in a wave of defections. However, as late as 1898 at least seventy-one clubs in Bradford were still playing Rugby Union. Only two clubs were reported to be playing under the auspices of the Northern Union outside the elite Yorkshire Senior Competition.

But alongside all this, a sea-change was brewing. Significantly, fifty-one clubs were already playing Association Football, as well as fourteen schools. Here was early evidence that a switch was beginning from rugby to football, marking a rejection of not just the Rugby Football Union but rugby in its entirety.

Although the majority of Northern Union clubs enjoyed increased profits during the inaugural season, expenditure on grounds and hidden payments to players ate into those profits. Bradford and Leeds, who had large capital investments in their grounds, faced an uphill battle to remain solvent. Success on the field was the only certain way of guaranteeing financial improvements. Manningham won the Northern Union's inaugural championship, winning the title on a dramatic last day of the season. The by now familiar formula for the victorious team - a parade through the streets - awaited Manningham on their return to Bradford. Around five thousand onlookers brought traffic to a standstill as players and officials appeared on the Belle Vue's balcony overlooking Manningham Lane. The biggest cheer came when George Lorimer, scorer of a third of the team's entire point total, took his turn to address the crowd.

And so it was that Bradford was to see a spectacle unlike anything that had gone before. For within a year, Manningham's championship-winning hero was dead of typhoid. George Lorimer passed away in the early hours of 8th February 1897 at the age of twenty-four. The massive reaction to his death speaks volumes about what rugby culture had become - in Bradford, in Manningham as both rugby club and community, and in the Northern Union game.

The untimely death of the hero resonates throughout human history. While we might expect a national figure, in that Victorian era of grandiosity, to have received a farewell of Homeric proportions, apparently those lower down the social scale could equally be bidden farewell with a lavish public commemoration. The 1890s have been described as the golden age of the Victorian funeral. Elaborate ceremonials of a kind which today would appear extravagant for a head of state were routine when burying a shop-keeper or a doctor. In London, as early as 1861 there is a record of an extraordinary funeral of a Fire Brigade superintendent who died in heroic circumstances, which celebrated the hero in the Carlylean mode on a scale as grand as any state or royal funeral.

Given the context, it would be surprising if a Victorian sporting personality did not have a lavish funeral. Indeed, many examples exist of enormous crowds attracted to sportsmen's funerals. Those of the Tyneside rowers Robert Chambers (1868), Harry Clasper (1870) and James Renforth (1871) were huge events with, in Clasper's case, a reported crowd of one hundred and thirty thousand lining the route of his funeral procession. Even modest sporting personalities could attract large crowds to their funerals: the 1891 burial of a potshare bowler attracted a thousand mourners from across Northumberland and County Durham, while the interment of Northumbrian pedestrian James Reay, killed in a mining accident in 1895, attracted five thousand people.

Although Lorimer was a regional, possibly national, sporting personality, his funeral was arguably a localised celebration of sport, place and identity. Lorimer had been living with his brother John, himself a former Manningham player, on Springcliffe Street, Manningham, a working-class terraced house in the shadow of the Manningham Mills complex. Eddie Holmes, the former Manningham captain and England international player, was appointed as the undertaker. Holmes's shop, on Oak Lane, was directly across the road from Manningham Mills and a short walk from the house where Lorimer died. The funeral on 10th February 1897 was described by the Bradford Daily Argus as 'a sad and imposing spectacle and probably such a sight has never been witnessed in Manningham'. The event was later called 'Manningham's state funeral'. As the procession made its way towards the cemetery, the roads were lined by upwards of eight thousand onlookers.

The wending of Lorimer's funeral procession around the streets of Manningham, passing the area's major employer, Lister Mills, showed clearly his central place in the everyday life of the community. The rugby club itself was by now self-evidently a part of the community's fabric and as such, a vehicle of local identity.

The fact that the funeral was on a similar scale to that of the industrialist and former lord mayor and MP Titus Salt must say something about the importance and popularity of rugby football in 1890s Bradford. In what might be viewed as a symbolic moment of identity, eight of Lorimer's team-mates carried his coffin to the graveside wearing claret and amber badges made of crepe and ribbons, and after the coffin was lowered into the ground, they dropped the badges one by one into the open grave.

Of course, the entrepreneurial types stepped in, always spotting an opportunity. The Victorians produced an endless list of keepsakes related to death, so it is unsurprising that a specially-produced Baines memorial card marked Lorimer's demise. The commercial exploitation of his death was far from unique; rower James Renforth's passing was marked by the production of dinner plates, glass eggs and photographs. There was even a suggestion that the public be charged sixpence to view Renforth's body.

While the lavish funeral procession was not uncommon in Victorian society, the newspapers' reports that such a sight had not been witnessed in Manningham before suggest that something out of the ordinary did occur, the day Lorimer was carried to his final resting place. The lavishness of the event surely wasn't entirely on the initiative of his family. In the wake of rugby's recent and still very raw split, was the pomp and circumstance with which the Northern Union saw its fallen hero to his grave an affirmation of the new code's proud survival?

For the Manningham club, the funeral allowed a final chance to use Lorimer's prowess as a statement of independence and status. Although their rival and neighbour, Bradford RFC, was heavily represented among those paying their respects, the dropping of claret and amber rosettes into the open grave was a display of pride and permanence. Was Manningham using the ceremony to construct a history? Reaffirm an identity? Perhaps most of all, the funeral, occurring just as rugby was teetering on the apex of its popularity before the incursions of football began in earnest, illustrated the enormous popularity of rugby and its centrality to society at that time, in life and even in death.

During the summer following the funeral (1897), Manningham Rugby Football Club redeveloped Valley Parade into one of the 'most commodious grounds in the county'. The club had taken on the debt of the ground's redevelopment immediately after winning the Northern Union championship. There must have been an expectation that success on the field would continue. But almost immediately, a combination of poor results and the success of their neighbours, the Bradford club, placed pressure on Manningham's finances. In an attempt to reduce costs, the club cut the tea allowance due to each second team player by sixpence. Five players went on strike. After a crisis meeting, the second XV accepted the club's position that the allowances had to be reduced due to the expenditure lavished on the ground.

But the finances continued to look grim. Manningham's 1898 annual meeting was informed that the club had lost £126. Gate receipts were down 15%. The main causes for the losses were a slow start in the league, early exit from the cup, and Bradford challenging for the title until the last game of the season. It was an early indication that success at Park Avenue could have a direct impact on the finances at Valley Parade. The following season was even more challenging. The 1899 annual meeting heard that £333 had been lost on the season. Debts now stood at £750.

Change was needed if the club were to remain viable. Local businessman Alfred Ayrton pushed through alterations to the running of the club. Every area of expenditure was examined, but Ayrton's new regime attracted bitter complaints that the club was being run 'on the cheap', with a Bradford Daily Telegraph correspondent accusing the club of being 'penny wise and pound foolish'. More worryingly, the rugby on show was said to be the 'worst ever'. The committee fought back, pointing to a healthier balance of £361, a stark contrast to the £400 loss the previous season. However, despite the prudence, the club was still £501 in debt.

The following season was every bit as disappointing. Even cup rugby could not tempt the crowds back to Valley Parade. A mere thousand folk turned up for the first round tie with Castleford - the lowest ever for a cup-tie. By contrast the 1901 semi-final of the Bradford Association Cup attracted a crowd of three thousand to Valley Parade. The ground was never to be fully utilised for the rugby cup semi-finals and finals for which it had been optimistically redeveloped.

However, the ground's facilities were leased in May 1901 to what might be termed a 'travelling history show' - a touring show entitled 'Savage South Africa'. Five hundred actors, one hundred and fifty horses and some 'well-trained elephants' re-enacted scenes from the Boer War and South African life. The Bradford Daily Argus was astonished to note the presence of 'real Boers and African darkies' among the cast. More than twenty thousand people saw the spectacle in the first seven days of a three-week run.

But though this additional income was welcome, it could not hide a trend of increasing debt. Manningham's 1901 annual meeting heard that the club was now £707 in debt. The income for that year was £1,870, including gates receipts of £1,260 (the Bradford derby alone accounting for £296 of this), £275 rental from 'Savage South Africa', and £246 from memberships. Although the club actually made a £205 profit on the season, the interest on the £1,100 mortgage had not been paid, and this had increased the debt.

The income from the annual Bradford derby was clearly essential to the club's financial viability, so unsurprisingly, Manningham opposed the desire among a number of clubs to form a breakaway league from the Northern Union. Despite their expressed opposition, that same year (1901), twelve Yorkshire and Lancashire clubs formed the Northern Rugby League.

This was a distinct move from bad to worse: Manningham was now cast adrift in the Yorkshire Senior Competition. Bereft of matches against Bradford, Huddersfield and Halifax, there was little doubt that the club's financial position would further decline. Then the Northern Rugby League's introduction of two divisions in 1902 made Manningham's finances even more untenable. The increased travelling that the second division brought with it was a particular burden, and attendances were disappointing. Financial losses were widespread among all clubs: Bramley lost £158, Huddersfield £219, and Stockport was disbanded. At Manningham's next annual meeting (1902) the season's losses were announced. They topped two hundred pounds. Gate receipts had halved, and membership had fallen by a third. Secretary Sam Naylor said starkly, 'if they [the finances] did not alter, the club could not go on'.

But there seems to have been a certain circumspection going on in the club's management. Throughout this period of Manningham's greatest financial difficulty, the club had been developing close links with the local association football pioneers. Indeed, the Bradford & District League Champions, Girlington, had been allowed to play its home matches at Valley Parade during the 1901-2 season. That decision had been a controversial one, as it had meant disbanding the second team in order to make Valley Parade available on every other Saturday. Of course, the fact that the second team had lost £130 on the previous season may also have been a reason. But with the growing popularity of football, one wonders whether the club had an eye on the future?

8

A match made in heaven: trams and cricket

As football and rugby underwent dramatic changes, it might be easy to assume that cricket was by comparison an island of serenity, particularly when viewed through the prism of mid-week county matches and 'timeless' (as in, without a fixed end) international test matches. However, in the north and midlands, a vibrant culture of league cricket was emerging. As previously noted, the introduction in 1850 of the closure of workplaces on Saturdays from two o-clock meant that league matches, played on Saturday afternoons, were accessible to the working classes. These leagues were every bit as cut-and-thrust as their football and rugby counterparts, and Bradford's Cricket League ended up being one of the best in the world. Its huge success was facilitated by the humble tramcar.

At the end of the nineteenth century it was not just football and rugby that felt the impact of league systems. Club cricket took inspiration from, and shared much of the culture of, rugby's Yorkshire Senior Competition, and from around 1893, league cricket became an integral part of the sporting calendar in Bradford. The development of spectator sport would be incomplete without an examination of the growth of league cricket.

As in rugby and football, it was cup competitions that would prepare the ground for a move towards a system of cricket leagues. In Yorkshire the first cup competition was the Emsley Cup, inaugurated in Leeds in 1880. Shortly after, two cups appeared in the Bradford area: the Airedale Challenge Cup and the Josling Challenge Cup (both 1884). Although the Josling Cup appears to have lasted for only a single year, the Airedale Challenge Cup continued for at least a decade, and may well have been the inspiration for the formation of the Airedale & Wharfedale League in 1893.

Leagues brought order and structure to local cricket. A combination of unified start-times, independent umpires, and league tables that gave a clear indication of the form and standing of clubs, saw the leagues hailed as a great success. The punctual start-times were the key to the leagues becoming popular and accessible, because matches were fitted around the work and domestic commitments of the population.

As though a touch-paper had been lit, the early 1890s saw cricket leagues rapidly take off, with new leagues appearing almost simultaneously right across the north of England: the North East Lancashire League and South East Lancashire League (1890), Huddersfield & District (1891), the Lancashire League, Central Lancashire League and Ribblesdale League (1892), Central Yorkshire (1893), North Yorkshire & South Durham (1893), and the Halifax & District League (1894).

This expansion was matched in the Bradford district with the formation of the leagues of Airedale & Wharfedale (1893), Bradford District (1893), Keighley & District (1893), Low Moor & District (1895), West Bradford (1893), and West Yorkshire (1893). The new leagues appear to have been popular: two thousand spectators were reported at a West Yorkshire League match between Bowling Old Lane and Bradford.

1893 was a significant year in the formation of Bradford's cricket leagues. The majority of these would have resulted from meetings held in late 1892 which would surely have taken inspiration from the founding of rugby's Yorkshire Senior Competition only a few months previously. History shows that the football and rugby leagues directly inspired the establishment of leagues in other sports. Both the Football League and cricket's first ever league, the

Birmingham and District Cricket League, were formed in the second half of 1886.

Bradford again and again proves its exemplary significance as a place in which spectator sports took root and subsequently took off. In the realm of cricket, a league that was to become one of the best in the country was the Bradford League, formed in 1903.

The Bradford League evidently had a strong base on which to build: in 1902 thirteen leagues were regularly reported on in the city's press. The impetus for the formation of the Bradford League came from a core of clubs from the West Bradford League. Frustrated by what they perceived as poor crowds and the 'unfair allocation' of derby matches, they convened a meeting in September 1902 attended by twelve clubs: seven from the West Bradford League (Allerton, Clayton, Great Horton, Lidget Green, Manningham Mills, Queensbury and Thornton), three from the Bradford & District League (Bankfoot, Dudley Hill, Shelf), and two from the Airedale & Wharfedale League (Eccleshill and Undercliffe). From this group of clubs, the Bradford League was founded.

The league had to be highly localised, as the time between the ending of a Saturday morning at work and the start of a five-hour cricket match meant that time spent travelling had to be kept to a minimum to make a league a practical proposition. Arguably one of the key elements of the success of the Bradford League was that of connectivity. The rapid expansion and electrification of the Bradford Corporation Tramway network in the space of just four years (1898-02) facilitated rapid and cheap transportation to virtually every area of the city. Electric tramways became an element of people's civic identity, and represented a commitment to technological progress.

The icing on the cake for the league's success came when, in April 1903, just four months before the Bradford League commenced, fares were reduced. Most were a penny with a maximum fare of tuppence to any terminus. Of the twelve Bradford League clubs, all bar one were served by the tramway. The exception was Clayton; the village was, however, connected to the Great Northern Railway's line from Bradford Exchange to Halifax and Keighley. Additionally, the Lidget Green terminus of the Bradford tramway was only one mile from Clayton.

The equation of the new tramway links with the amazingly swift development of the Bradford League is given further credence by the fact that Saltaire and Windhill joined the league in 1905 following the absorption into the Bradford system of the Mid-Yorkshire Tramways that ran near both grounds. In 1912, a couple of years after the opening of the Pudsey tramway and the joining up of the Bradford and Leeds systems, there was an influx of clubs into the league from east of the city: Farsley, Laisterdyke, Pudsey Britannia, Pudsey St. Lawrence, and Stanningley & Farsley.

The popularity of the Bradford League was immense: the 1913 Priestley Cup Final was watched by thirteen thousand spectators, and in 1919, more people watched Bradford League matches (265,770) than those of the Yorkshire County Cricket Club. The popularity of league cricket in places such as Birmingham, Bradford, and Lancashire probably reflects the fact that clubs playing in such leagues were rooted in their communities and, in comparison to the county clubs, were easily accessible. These leagues made a strong contribution to working-class life. The clubs playing in the league and cup competitions provided a highly localised sense of identity and were vehicles for neighbourhood rivalries. Plus, with their Saturday afternoon schedules, the leagues effectively catered to football and rugby supporters by providing recreational spectating through the summer.

The Bradford League benefited from its association in people's minds with modernity due to its exploitation of the connectivity and convenience offered by the expanded tramway system. The League was furthermore asserting itself as an important element of civic identity. It was something else in which Bradford's working people could take pride. The timing had been perfect. On the back of a new and cheap form of public transport, Bradford cricket found itself on a roll.

Kick-off

9
The City of Bradford and Bradford City – a double birth

At the end of the nineteenth century, Bradford, 'worstedopolis' of the world, was entering its modern age. In 1897, city status was finally granted, and the modern city was born. Societal changes were inevitably reflected in the sporting landscape of the period. The city heralded the new century by embracing the national game of football. However, it was the rivalries born of Victorian rugby that would define Bradford's sports scene for over a century to come.

Bradford's new city status heralded an expansion of Bradford's boundaries to incorporate Allerton, Eccleshill, Heaton, Idle, North Bierley, Thornton, Tong, Tyersal and Wyke. Gas and electricity came under municipal control. Even death was municipalised when a public cemetery opened at Scholemoor. Bradford became the first place in Britain to provide school dinners to pupils. The water supply, essential for both the thirsty textile mills and an expanded population, was secured with the construction of large reservoirs in Nidderdale. But as we have seen regarding the exponential rise of cricket in this period, the thing that arguably had the greatest impact on the city's sporting life was its brand new tramway system which reached to, and beyond, Bradford's boundaries, bringing many new communities into the city's orbit.

In its heyday rugby had had an iron grip on Bradford, with at least one hundred and twenty rugby teams reportedly playing matches in the city in 1894. From this sheer scale, the game's fall in the wake of rugby's great split was dramatic. Not only did the Rugby Union lose high-profile gate-taking clubs such as Bradford and Manningham, the game also lost its grassroots - and thousands of its players. Shockingly, by the turn of the century, Rugby Union had virtually ceased to exist in West Yorkshire, with the Yorkshire Rugby Union declining at one stage to seven clubs.

The inverse trajectory of football is striking. The West Yorkshire Association League, founded in February 1894, commenced with only six clubs in its ranks. However, ten years later it had grown to 436 clubs, of which Bradford accounted for a quarter of the total. If the number of teams playing is any indication, it was not the Northern Union that benefitted from the intransigence of the Rugby Union, it was football. The sportsmen, and children, of Bradford turned their collective backs on not just Rugby Union, but rugby as a whole.

And what of women? As has been said, by the end of the nineteenth century women had largely retreated from spectatorship in both codes of football. The primacy of male leisure, particularly in working-class households, must have been a significant driver of this decline. Bradford's men spent the 'leisure money' – even though in West Yorkshire (and East Lancashire) records show that, in that period, an unusually strong contribution to household incomes was being made by the womenfolk due to their employment in the mills.

As social historian Brad Beaven concludes from his comprehensive research into the era, 'it was working class males, free from the difficulties of balancing the family budget, who were the true beneficiaries of the economic circumstances of the late nineteenth century'. Basically the Saturday match was part of an uncheckable male culture of escapism from the household, a culture which some might say has survived intact to the present day. Did women back then, left with all child-rearing and housekeeping responsibilities, get a look-in on the new phenomenon of 'leisure'?

A brief diversion into the fledgling beginnings of women's participation in football as players partly addresses that question. It was the First World War (1914-18) that transformed women's football. Over one million women would enter the workplace to fill the jobs vacated by men who'd gone to fight. The cultural impact of this empowerment of women who still did not even have the right to vote cannot be overstated.

During the Great War women's football rocketed to popularity as a spectator sport. The linkage with the war, and the fact that the game had a social purpose (charity fund-raising), enabled women's football to side-step the constraints imposed by gender stereotyping. In particular, the tapping into the narrative of the 'plucky heroine' as women were thrown into traditional male roles at home, in the work place and on the sports field meant that games during this era avoided condescending and hostile perceptions that have otherwise dogged women's football. It has been argued that spectators were more receptive because the matches were charitable events that raised money for the families of soldiers killed or wounded at the front.

But how did this astonishing phenomenon so quickly come about? The wartime government recommended the encouragement of sporting activities among women entering physically demanding industries. A bunch of women nick-named the 'munitionettes' (women working in munitions factories producing shells, bullets, and bombs) took up football with such zeal that it almost became their official sport. The munitionettes were a highly visible advertisement for women's football, hence many other industries that employed large numbers of women also quickly spawned teams.

Bradford's women were naturally in thrall! Manningham Ladies was formed in 1921 from Lister's Mill workers, the bulk of the team being made up of Lister's Mill hockey team. Straight off, in April of that year, they famously played Dick Kerr's Ladies at Valley Parade to raise money for charity. This early team then disbanded, but it appears to have been the inspiration behind the formation that same month of another Bradford-based team, Hey's Ladies, made up of workers from Hey's Brewery on Lumb Lane, Manningham. Shortly after that, the inaugural meeting of the English Ladies' Football Association took place in the city, and Bradford became in the early 'twenties, for a brief and intense period, something of a centre for women's football, mainly due to the prowess of Hey's Ladies.

But this flurry of women's football was confined to a handful of years, owing largely to a nationwide ban issued by the Football Association in December 1921 to stop women from playing on any Football League grounds. This would have made life very difficult for the new teams, faced with the interminable problem of finding a suitable ground whenever they wanted to play a match.

And now back to 1890s Bradford, where, albeit *sans* women's participation, football's advance was unstoppable. Though the expansion of football in Bradford in the early years of the twentieth century would be rapid, it could draw on many continuities as it sought to establish itself: the folk or street heritage of football; rivalries produced when streets, communities and towns were pitted against one another in sports such as club cricket; strong commercial and cultural parallels with rugby. Additionally, during the 1860s and 1870s several West Riding rugby clubs played association football, or variants of it, in their formative years. Thus, like rugby before it, football was not an alien game thrust upon an ignorant public; it arrived into an environment where the ingredients existed for it to thrive.

The first sustained attempt to establish football in the city came with the formation of Bradford Association Football Club (AFC) in August 1895. The club became the association football section of the Park Avenue-based Bradford Cricket, Athletic & Football Club – the football club in the title referring in fact to the famous rugby club. Some of the Bradford AFC players were said to be workmen whose trades had called them from Scotland, Lancashire and the midlands to work in Bradford – more evidence that Bradford was not insulated from the national influence of football.

In their inaugural season, Bradford AFC won the West Yorkshire League title, the Leeds Hospital Cup, and played in front of attendances ranging between two and three thousand. For the 1897-8 season Bradford AFC joined the Yorkshire League which was dominated by second XIs of South Yorkshire clubs. Bradford lost twelve of their eighteen games and conceded seventy-seven goals. The momentum of the club appears to have been lost when the football club was relocated, for the 1898-9 season, to the Birch Lane ground in West Bowling. Attendances declined to around the five hundred mark. That, allied to disinterest, possibly even hostility, from the dominant rugby section, and also financial losses, resulted in Bradford's pioneering football club being disbanded in 1899.

Ironically, the disbandment of Bradford AFC, and neighbouring Bowling AFC, gave local football a timely boost. As a Bradford Daily Telegraph article noted, at the end of the 1899-1900 season several clubs were short of players. However, the distribution of the players of the two disbanded clubs around the various other local clubs gave football in Bradford a new lease of life. One major beneficially was Girlington. The club took on many of the released players and, featuring what could have been semi-professional players in the shape of Fletcher (formerly of Scarborough) and Geordie Hubbert (Glasgow Rangers), Girlington twice won the Bradford & District League in 1900 and 1901.

Another massive boost for football in the city was the Schools' Association's abandonment of rugby for football in 1895. As we've seen in many other sports, a cup competition was often a central part of popularising a game, and football was no exception. The donation of the Bradford Cup by former Bradford AFC player

Colonel Armitage was an important stepping stone to the establishment of nearly a hundred schools and junior teams in the city. From September 1902 onwards, news reports show a sea change in the sporting habits of Bradfordians. Ninety-two football clubs were by now competing in four leagues with a total of nine divisions and eighteen school teams playing in a two-division league.

Football's nationalisation was greatly aided by the spread of the game at schoolboy level. Of course the schools themselves, following the 1880 Education Act, were part of the nationalisation of British society. Bradford was in the vanguard of provision of free primary education for all, with many of the original 'Board School' buildings still standing today. In these mixed schools, both girls and boys took part in Physical Education. This did not, however, have the effect of bringing women into greater prominence in the city's sporting life.

The Bradford Schools' Athletic Association (BSAA) was formed in 1892. For the first three years of its existence the BSAA organised games of rugby; however, in 1895 football came to replace rugby. Several histories of football in Bradford have quoted a boy breaking his leg playing rugby during the 1895-6 season as the reason for the switch to football, though this might be apocryphal (in the centenary history of the BSAA, doubt is expressed about one accident being the cause of the switch).

Of course, the adoption of football dovetails with the great split that led to the formation of the Northern Union. It is impossible to know whether the schoolmasters were disillusioned with the actions of the Rugby Union, the Northern Union or indeed rugby in general. However, that one broken leg may have offered a timely excuse for the switch. The Bradford Observer wrote that 'the teachers believed [that soccer] would be more convenient, and besides would be more acceptable to the parents of the boys'.

By 1900 twenty schools were competing in the BSAA football league. Accidents aside, there were several factors that probably helped facilitate the change of codes. Football was relatively inexpensive, and for an urban school the adaptability of the game was ideal for cramped playgrounds with hard surfaces. The inclusivity of football to boys of all physical sizes made the game attractive in comparison to the greater physical demands of rugby that would favour stronger and larger boys. Need it be said that in British society at the turn of the nineteenth century, the participation of girls in such field sports, whether in or out of school, was totally off the agenda. Or might it be that some individuals muscled in on street kick-abouts with the boys?

There is evidence that besides a top-down spread of football, boys also organised their own clubs. The author J.B. Priestley, born in Manningham in 1894, played full back in school matches. He also played for the neighbourhood team Toller Lane Tykes, and was photographed in 1905 with his friends and their invented Saltburn United AFC – the name being a reference to Saltburn Place where the Priestley family lived. Priestley's boyhood teams may be reflective of the 'football craze' among boys during the period. This was represented by seemingly continuous games of street football with the loose teams offering the boys a sense of a highly localised identity. The formalising of street-corner sides, whose intimate connection with everyday life is reflected in their names, could be seen as the link, or transition, between the world of the child and adult. These clubs were arguably the basic unit of the sporting landscape.

After schools' football, probably the most critical factor in translating the local enthusiasm for football into the establishment of a professional football club was the persistent lobbying of the soccer correspondent of the newspaper the Yorkshire Sports. The press's influence was highly significant. Two of the foremost pioneers in establishing a professional football club in Bradford were the sub-editor of the Bradford Observer, James Whyte, who had played football in his native Scotland, and the headmaster of St Jude's School and former Stoke City player, John Brunt.

Regionally, one of the most widely read sporting newspapers was the (Manchester-based) Athletic News. With a claimed circulation of 180,000 by the 1890s, and with its northern and midlands focus, its influence must have been great. Although Athletic News covered a myriad of sports, there is little doubt that it was strongly identified with professional football; in fact its editor between 1893 and 1900 was the president of the Football League. Hence as the case for a professional football club in Bradford was made, Athletic News' reporting on the situation was, at the very least, extremely well informed and was probably almost a running commentary from a Football League perspective.

The opening days of 1903 saw a concerted attempt to form a professional football club in the city. A circular written by Whyte and Brunt claimed, as a 'moderate estimate', that twenty thousand spectators watched local association games on any given Saturday. With that figure in mind, they suggested that a professional team would attract seven or eight thousand supporters. In late January, Athletic News, commenting on the possibility of a professional team in West Yorkshire, signalled what could be viewed as explicit support from football's governing bodies and League clubs:

It is believed that the first in the field will receive most consideration and greatest assistance from the Football Association. It is said that some of the clubs with more professionals than they require are willing to grant transfers without payment of the usual fees, and there is a strong belief that the first professional team formed in that particular district will be given a place in the Second Division ... with a view to fostering the "Socker" code at a more rapid rate than would possibly be the case if the team had to fight its way through the ordinary channels.

In late January 1903 Whyte and Brunt were invited to a meeting at Valley Parade by Manningham's president Alfred Ayrton. There, for the first time, the possibility of a professional football club was discussed. The following month a committee was formed to begin the detailed planning required to bring a professional football club to fruition. By the end of the month they had secured support from enough Football League sides to be able to state 'should a club be formed, little doubt now exists as to the question of securing admission to the second division of the Football League'. The case for a new professional club in Bradford continued to be made via the pages of the Athletic News. In mid-March a letter was reproduced stating that there was already in place a *well-equipped ground, capable of accommodating 25,000 spectators; dressing rooms and bath rooms on the ground; a capital of between £2,500 and £3,000 with which to begin operations of securing a really capable team.*

Hence a special meeting of Manningham members was held before the end of that month – at which it was heard that over the last three years, nearly a thousand pounds had been lost. The previous Saturday, £115 had been taken at the gate for the derby against Keighley, a sum that was ten times greater than at least half a dozen other games that season. With Keighley and Leeds poised for promotion to the first division, those lucrative paydays would be lost. The football pioneers were offering to provide £2,000 cash (albeit repayable at 5% interest) if Manningham would offer the ground and £500 capital.

After two hours of debate, the meeting gave overwhelming support to 'form a first class football team to be run in conjunction with the present rugby team'. In reply to a question from the floor, Ayrton said the new club was to be called 'Bradford City Football Club'.

It was claimed that eighteen Football League clubs were supportive of the emerging Bradford bid for Football League status, and in April both Middlesbrough and Sheffield United sent teams to play exhibition games that attracted a total of nine thousand spectators. The Athletic News wrote: *The fact that it is possible to arrange such matches may be accepted as evidence, first of a willingness of League clubs to lend a helping hand to a new district, and next to the ability of the football public in that district to make each game pay.*

At the Football League's next Annual General Meeting (25th May 1903), Bradford City was voted into the league by an overwhelming majority, with thirty of thirty-three Football League clubs supporting the new club. Their presence in rugby-dominated West Yorkshire was undoubtedly attractive, as the area had already demonstrated that it could generate large gate-paying crowds for rugby matches, and Bradford was within easy travelling distance of the majority of Football League clubs. However, the election of Bradford City to the League, rather than being part of a 'colonisation' policy, may have been simply that clubs from areas with small populations were sacrificed by the Football League in order to raise overall attendances for what might be described as a sporting cartel. It appears that the events of 1903 were part of an incremental expansion that was preferable both geographically and financially to a bolder strategic inclusion of a club from London and or the south.

One obstacle remained to the establishment of a professional football club: the members of Manningham rugby club. As a democratic organisation they had the power to kill the infant club at birth. Four days after the Football League voted Bradford in, the Manningham club's annual meeting heard that they had lost £609 on the season. Only an athletics festival had saved the club. It had grossed £1,772, which had cleared the club's debts and left a balance at hand of £472. President Alfred Aryton concluded that Manningham could not survive as a second division rugby club.

He urged the members to support 'a game that would pay'. Although a call for rugby to be retained was 'met with great cheers', after a further two hours of debate, it was agreed by seventy-five to thirty-four votes that rugby would be abandoned.

And so Bradford City Association Football Club (AFC) was born.

KICK-OFF

10
Football comes to Valley Parade

Bradford City AFC became the only side to join the Football League without having played a match of any description. The size of the task facing the infant club during its first season in the Football League should not be underestimated. It was without precedent, and represented a huge gamble for not only the football club, but also the Football League itself.

The pressures of competing in a truly national competition were considerable. While gate receipts were five times higher than the final season in the Northern Union, the player costs were six times higher and the travel costs four times greater. Reducing player costs by producing their own players was difficult, given the relative short history of the game in the district. One issue was the inability of the club's reserve players to bridge the gulf in class between the West Yorkshire League (which they won) and, when injuries required it, a place in the first team. Against such a backdrop, it was a great achievement when Bradford City's first season in the Football League resulted in a mid-table finish and the posting of a small financial profit.

Success was the only certain way of improving finances, but the pursuit of success cost money, and in their second season, 1904-5, a loss of £440 was reported. Although overheads were greater, so was the income. Gate receipts of £635 for the home FA Cup tie against Wolverhampton Wanderers in February 1906, with a crowd of seventeen thousand, exceeded those taken in the whole of the club's final season in the Northern Union.

However, the club continued to makes losses, and when a £2,000 'trading deficiency' was announced, a commission of inquiry into the club's financial structure was formed. Their recommendations saw the club registered as a limited company. The financial restructuring of the club and the appointment of Peter O'Rourke as secretary-manager were critical decisions in the club's history. Thankfully, O'Rourke led City to a fifth place finish in 1906-7 which resulted in record gate receipts and the overall bank overdraft being halved.

Promotion to Division One in 1908 dovetailed with the establishment of the limited company. The share issue was expected to raise the necessary finance to expand Valley Parade for first division crowds and bring in players capable of retaining the club's top-flight status. The poor take-up of the £1 shares - little more than half of the seven thousand total – was disappointing. The redevelopment of Valley Parade had cost £10,000, so the club was left under-capitalised and dependent on income at the gate.

However, it was nothing short of astonishing that in a mere five seasons, Bradford City had established themselves as a Football League side and gained promotion to the first division. Between 1908 and the outbreak of the Great War they would go on to become one of the leading clubs in the country and would win the FA Cup in 1911. The magnitude of Bradford City's success must be classed as the major factor in the successful establishment of football in West Yorkshire. Without that sure first step, the subsequent professional club formations at Leeds, Huddersfield and Halifax may not have been made with such confidence. Bradford City's success led to an irrevocable alteration of the sporting landscape of West Yorkshire, and nowhere would that be felt more keenly than in the board room of Bradford Rugby Football Club at Park Avenue.

It is ironic that the Bradford RFC committee were initially delighted by Manningham's conversion to football. They expected disenfranchised rugby supporters to rally behind Bradford RFC. Initially the prospects looked bright for Bradford as they found success on the field, winning the Northern Union championship in 1904, ending as runners-up in 1905 and lifting the Challenge Cup in 1906. However, across Yorkshire football's inexorable rise was impacting hard on rugby club finances. In 1903 the Yorkshire Post doubted whether any second tier side had made rugby pay. Perhaps most significantly, Holbeck RFC's defeat in a promotion play-off match at the end of the 1903-4 season left the club facing another season in the second tier of the Northern Union. Members of the club pushed for a switch to the association game. As Leeds was the biggest city in England without a Football League club, the prospect of success seemed to be excellent. Thus the rugby club's Elland Road ground became the home of Leeds City AFC, and professional football was brought to Bradford's neighbouring city for the 1904-5 season.

Rugby was now in crisis. Between 1904 and 1907 at Batley, Castleford, Keighley, Leigh and Swinton, players accepted pay cuts due to the dire economic positions of their clubs. In early 1907 the Keighley News summed up the enormous impact that the rise of football was having on the Northern Union game:

The rapid march of the association code has undoubtedly put the rugby popularity in the shade – 17,000 at Bradford City last week, while 2,000 watched a big rugby match ... Within the past ten years the following clubs have dropped out of existence. Bingley, Shipley, Keighley Olicana, Cross Roads, Keighley Clarence, Keighley St. Annes, Silsden, Haworth, Denholme, Pudsey, Todmorden, Goole, Outwood, Kinsley, Heckmondwike, Holbeck, Windhill, Cleckheaton, Eastmoor, Bowling, Luddendenfoot, Normanton, Rothwell, Brighouse Rangers, Liversedge, Castleford, Alverthorpe, Otley, Featherstone, Elland, Idle, Morley, Pontefract, Hull Marlboro, Ripon, Leeds Parish Church, Manningham, Ossett, Hebden Bridge and Kirkstall.

Thus it was that Bradford RFC's Park Avenue ground, the physical embodiment of civic pride, was becoming an unsustainable liability. The ground had been lavishly developed in competition with other Yorkshire towns in an effort to be the most prestigious sporting amenities in Yorkshire. The development had come with a high price tag, and in 1896 it was reported that £10,300 was owed. Despite profits in all but one of the club's seasons in the Northern Union, more than a decade later £7,000 was still owed. In 1906-7 Bradford RFC finished in eighteenth place in the new single division Northern Union, bringing the worst financial result in the club's history. Bradford CA&FC had lost £770 on all sports.

Selling the loss-making cricketing field was impossible, as the land was subject to a ninety-nine year lease stipulating that it could only be utilised for sporting purposes. However, even had that option been available, the club would not have contemplated selling the cricket ground as it would have impacted badly on the prestige and civic standing of the town. Bradford's president Harry Briggs concluded that rugby could not generate the income required to service the club's debts, and that only a Football League club could.

11
Sport at war: rugby vs football

The successful introduction of professional football at Valley Parade placed Bradford sport onto the national stage. In contrast to the geographically constrained Northern Union, Bradford City's trials and tribulations in the Football League were often national news. Sport had in some respects caught up with the wider city. Edwardian Bradford entered the new century enjoying its status as one of the world's leading industrial centres. This was epitomised by the Bradford Exhibition of 1904, through which the city presented itself to the world as an industrious, respectable, self-confident and altogether massively successful metropolis.

The Bradford Exhibition was opened by the Prince and Princess of Wales (the future King George V and Queen Mary) in May 1904. Held in Lister Park, the centre-piece was a specially built sixty thousand square foot Industrial Hall that displayed textile goods and machinery; engineering products including locomotion, sanitation, general and domestic; and a women's section. A large concert hall offered orchestral bands, hand-bell ringers, glee parties and military bands. It also accommodated an educational conference, a grocers' exhibition and conference, and a schools' exhibition. In the park's grounds were a model hospital, botanical displays, a Somali village, Palace of Illusions, Crystal Maze and a shooting range. A motor launch and a Venetian gondola shared the park lake with a naval spectacle that included scenes from the bombardment of Port Arthur, the siege of which was still an ongoing part of the Russo-Japanese War.

The exhibition was an unqualified success, with going on for two and a half million people passing through the gates. It was a proclamation that Bradford's journey from market town to one of the world's leading industrial cities was complete.

Local pride and identity are recurring themes throughout this tale of the growth of spectator sports. Sporting clubs have always been focal points of these dimensions of working people's lives, and this localism is the thread that explains and stitches together most of the events of this chapter.

The highly localised nature of football support in the decades prior to the Great War is due in part (prior to the spread of tramways) to the majority of working-class supporters walking to home matches. Those supporters provided the backbone of the club's support, and they could come to dominate and shape the self-image of the club. Even after the development of urban tramways, cities such as Birmingham, Liverpool, Manchester and Sheffield were as much divided as united by football loyalties.

Among diverse populations such as Bradford's, football fostered an attachment to place that no other form of social citizenship achieved. The importance of this is that, once club loyalties have been carefully constructed, they are stubbornly difficult to unravel. This appears to be particularly the case from the 1900s onwards. Sport and its place in wider society had apparently become more stable, perhaps showing that British industrial towns and cities had themselves arrived at a point in their development when rapid changes to the geography and population had stabilised, allowing the emergence of a civic society. Football, it has been said, gave working-class males a sense of identity through a feeling of 'local' patriotism, fuelled by their attachment to their working-class environments. This being the case, it is no surprise that successful football club mergers are notable by their rarity.

So when, in 1907, a merger was suggested between Bradford City and Bradford (Park Avenue), it was like seeking the impossible: the bringing together of two organisations that had fought for civic sporting supremacy since the 1880s. Throughout their previous incarnations as rugby clubs, both had won major trophies and had attracted crowds in the tens of thousands. Bradford (Park Avenue) had been formed partly due to frustration with the low social standing that competing in the Northern Union offered the once imperious Bradford club. The club enjoyed impressive facilities and a very strong sense of their history and identity, its ownership structure dominated by factory owner and former Rugby Union player with the Bradford club, Harry Briggs. The chimney of his Briggella Mills was clearly visible from Park Avenue. He owned factories in Poland and Russia, saw-mills in Hull, and introduced Mr Rolls to Mr Royce (later becoming a director of Rolls Royce). Across the city at Valley Parade, the Bradford City members were mistrustful of the management structure at Park Avenue and Briggs's central and at times autocratic role.

Rumours of a merger between the Park Avenue based Bradford RFC and Bradford City AFC surfaced as early as 1905. The Bradford Daily Argus opined that 'the thousands of City followers up Manningham way would set up a perfect howl of opposition'. From the first, the debate was being driven by identities formed by Victorian rugby rivalries. The passions behind those identities were vividly displayed at a meeting of Bradford City members. It was dominated by the rumours of a move to Park Avenue. An official stated 'every member was deadly opposed to the removal of the club from Manningham'. The comment that the club would not be 'removed from Manningham' indicates that, despite switching sports to become Bradford City AFC, the identity of the club was still strongly anchored to the club's rugby past and its geographical home in Manningham.

A series of letters - probably designed to exert pressure on the Bradford City committee - had appeared in the press stating that the Park Avenue club was willing to spend £5,000 to set up a professional football team. A three month rolling lease on City's Valley Parade ground, allied to the engineering challenge of developing the steeply sloping site, forced the City committee to inspect sites for a new ground, including one at Briggella Mills, Little Horton Lane, owned by none other than Bradford RFC chairman Harry Briggs. His attendance at Bradford City's game with Glossop North End in October sent the rumour mill into overdrive. The Bradford Daily Argus observed, *If only the old parochial sentiment of 'Manningham' could be forgotten and the club merged with Bradford, the course of events would lead straightaway to success equalling anything known in the past.*

The Argus also revealed that Bradford had already lost £500 on the season, and that was projected to double by the season's end. However, despite the hefty mortgage on the ground, the property assets on the Park Avenue estate were such that it was thought sufficient funds could be found to set up a professional football team. The Bradford RFC committee was convinced that the quality of a bid for Football League membership would be such that it would overcome the reluctance to have two Bradford clubs in the second division.

In early 1907 an open letter to Bradford City, almost certainly written by a Bradford RFC committee member, appeared in the press. It appealed for City to take a broad view when considering an amalgamation. The response was immediate, with one correspondent proclaiming, *Amalgamation of the two clubs is impossible as the old Manningham sentiment still strongly prevails [...] Two clubs could not possibly be made to pay. Bradford should either adopt Rugby Union or let the ground to Bradford City.*

The following Saturday Charles Sutcliffe of the Football League management committee attended Bradford City's FA Cup tie against Reading and told the press, *there will soon be soccer at Park Avenue and I venture that Bradford City will supply the football desired.*

Until then they must be satisfied to plug away at Valley Parade, which some day will be regarded as a mere matchbox ground, for the City people are all ambition and enthusiasm.

On 14 January 1907 the Bradford RFC property and finance committee met. They had taken a meagre £28 on the gate for the visit of Huddersfield to Park Avenue in the Northern Union, whilst across the city a crowd of eighteen thousand had witnessed Bradford City's FA Cup victory over Reading. They discussed several future paths: seek alterations to the rules of the Northern Union game to make it more like the Rugby Union of old; continue with Northern Union working closely with the junior game in the city; form a professional football club.

It is difficult to fully explain Bradford's demands for a return to Rugby Union rules. Did they imagine that a reversion to Rugby Union rules, and a potential *rapprochement* with the RFU, would bring back the crowds to Park Avenue? Or was this the engineering of a dispute that would be impossible to resolve, thus leaving the way clear for a departure from the Northern Union and the establishment of a professional football club? In the wake of the meeting, Harry Briggs issued an ultimatum that strongly suggests the club was set on a path outside the Northern Union:

If the Northern Union authorities do not revert to the Rugby Union game by the end of the season, we must sever our connection with the Northern Union. Since 1903 there has been a steady decrease of public support, amounting to some 50% and this season average gates of £39 have resulted in a £500 loss so far. We have been saved from actual loss in the intervening years by good fortune in the cup, but that is too precarious a source upon which to stake the existence of an institution like Park Avenue. It would be ruinous to go on increasing our liabilities in connection with a game which the public, here at any rate, will not support.

Three weeks later, sixty people 'of all shades of rugby opinion' met at the Osbourne Hotel. They decided to attempt to convene a meeting of Bradford CA&FC guinea members, to pass a resolution to restore voting rights for the half-guinea members. The hope, presumably, was that the popular vote would back the retention of Northern Union rugby at Park Avenue.

However, the old guard was gathering support for a reversion to Rugby Union. A month later (10th March) the former Bradford Rugby Football Club favourite, Tom Broadley, hosted a meeting. His team-mates Fred Bonsor and Laurie Hickson also gave public backing for a return to the old game. That view received strong support when Syd Wray, the honorary secretary of the Yorkshire Rugby Union, proposed that Bradford return to the fold. Hickson told the local press he had received *most encouraging communications from leading officials. It was not unlikely that they would be able to obtain the north v south match of next season and most, if not all, county matches.*

The Athletic News, while agreeing that there was 'certainly room for a good amateur rugby club in Bradford', doubted 'whether such a club could successfully flourish if saddled with the dimensions of Park Avenue'. A further hurdle was that before Bradford could be allowed back into the Rugby Football Union, the entire Bradford committee would be expected to resign as a first step towards reinstatement. Bradford committee member Fred Lister not surprisingly dismissed the proposal as 'retrograde and not likely to be attended with financial success'. He went onto say that the two hundred replies to the circular sent out to members had been 'four to one in favour of association football'. The Bradford Daily Argus commented that the most significant development thus far was that the proposal to convene a meeting in order to bring back voting rights for the half-guinea members was still lying idle on the Bradford committee's table, implying that the committee did not want the option of remaining part of the Northern Union to be available.

Bradford City's fabulous form at the end of the 1906-7 season made promotion to the first division seem a real possibility; some were describing it as a certainty. Huge crowds had packed Valley Parade, and there seemed to be no end in sight to the football boom in the city. In such a climate, many asked why Bradford City should even consider amalgamation. City's weakness was the three month rolling lease on Valley Parade from the Midland Railway Company. Unless a long lease could be agreed, the financial case for the huge investment the ground needed to host first division football was difficult to make. An amalgamation with Bradford RFC would provide Bradford City with virtually a readymade ground. However, if both clubs' existing mortgages were added together, and the costs of expanding Park Avenue for first division football added on, something in the order of £12,000 would be required to get the new venture off the ground.

Another month, another meeting. But this one was to be exhaustive and momentous. The guinea members of Bradford RFC met at the bowling green pavilion on the evening of Monday 15th April with the Lord Mayor of Bradford, J.A. Godwin, president of the club, chairing. When asked whether the outcome of the meeting would be 'taken as final', the mayor consulted with the committee then stated that the result would indeed be 'final and binding'. The accounts of the club were examined and showed a steady decline. In 1903-4 the profit had been £702, but in 1904-5 this had fallen to £66. President Harry Briggs, absent due to a 'medical condition', said in a letter to the members that attendances had halved and only good fortune in the cup had saved the club from heavy losses: 'with the advent of association football in our city, the spectators had been drawn from rugby'. He concluded that only football could make Park Avenue a financial success.

The question came – had any agreement been made with Bradford City? The lord mayor answered, 'no overtures have been made, and I do not think we should complicate this question with the idea of any amalgamation'. Another member asked if the committee had considered forming their own professional football team at Park Avenue. Major Shepherd replied 'there is no attempt, at present, to try and get into the second league'. It was suggested that the meeting be postponed, since only the club's guinea members were being allowed to vote on the club's future. The lord mayor said that legally the constitution of the club was in the hands of the guinea members alone, and ruled the request out of order. Club membership was in three categories: 500 guinea members, 200 half-guinea members and 130 life members. Thus around a quarter of the club's membership were denied a vote.

Three options were put forward: continue another season of the Northern Union game? Go back to Rugby Union? Adopt the Association game?

The motion to stay with the Northern Union was well supported, but to contemptuous cries, not a single committee member backed the proposal. The motion to revert to Rugby Union attracted a minority, until a member shouted 'rugby of any kind', which encouraged a majority to show their hands. The motion to switch to football attracted fewer votes than both rugby votes combined.

To gain some much-needed clarity, a proposal was put forward that a vote should be taken on whether the club should adopt rugby or football. This vote went ahead, and a considerable majority voted in favour of rugby. With that settled, a further vote was taken: Rugby Union, or Northern Union? When a sizeable majority voted for a reversion to Rugby Union, the mayor pronounced, 'the old game has it'.

12
'Ruinous departures': the triumph of tribalism

And so, on the morning of Tuesday 16th April 1907, Bradford Rugby Football Club's members and supporters woke up to the news that any thoughts of adopting football had been comprehensively defeated, and furthermore, the club was abandoning the Northern Union and returning to Rugby Union.

However, Harry Briggs kicked off the day with controversy by immediately telling the local press that the outcome of the meeting was 'illegal'! He claimed they had only met to consider and recommend a course of action, and said he was satisfied that under the circumstances, he was justified in the interests of the club and the wider community of Bradford in taking action against what he saw as a 'ruinous departure'.

Briggs said he would call a further meeting and ballot *all* the club's members, so the ultimate decision would truly represent the club. Only then would he be happy to accept the result. Of the previous night's meeting, Briggs said, 'the mayor had not quite realised the importance of the three points of issue', and claimed that 'not only did some members vote for both codes [of rugby], but some held up both hands'. Widening his criticism, Briggs thought that many at Valley Parade 'would be glad at the turn of events', but cautioned against any triumphalism by stating that 'Park Avenue must inevitably regain its pre-eminence in the city'. He was however, agreeable that if football was decided on, there should be an amalgamation with Bradford City. But, if City approached negotiations with the assumption that Bradford must be bottom dog, he would advocate that Bradford 'go in [to football] on their own'. Diplomacy evidently was not Briggs's strongest point. In view of these sentiments, the first season's result of a mid-table finish and (albeit modest) profit for Bradford City was, as previously noted, a great achievement.

The Bradford Daily Argus commented that it seemed odd that a gathering of illustrious citizens including two reverends and several councillors, overseen by none other than the lord mayor, had managed to hold an 'illegal' meeting. Apparently, the regulation that only the finance and property committee was able to call a meeting of members had only been noticed after the meeting and its unexpected outcome. The writer concluded that the only dignified course of action was for the entire committee to resign. This, of course, did not happen.

Two days later Bradford RFC's Harry Briggs and Horace Geldard met Bradford City AFC chairman, Colonel Armitage. The Bradford Daily Argus now overflowed with optimism: *Quite apart from mere local sentiment, there is a desire to settle on eminently reasonable lines. It may almost be written that there will be Bradford City at Park Avenue next season and a Bradford club in the first division within two years.*

That 'mere local sentiment' was soon in evidence. The Argus reported a 'spirit of keen resentment' among Bradford City members. The widespread view was that Bradford RFC was jealous of Bradford City's success and wanted to swallow them up. Bradford RFC would thus be rescued overnight from years of muddle, and be transformed into one of the leading football teams in the land. So great was the animosity to this that a hard core of Bradford City fans even talked of forming a new football club at Valley Parade if the amalgamation went ahead.

A series of letters hostile to the amalgamation appeared in the local press. 'It is the old spirit of lordly Park Avenue and lowly Valley Parade', railed one correspondent, and another, 'however distasteful it maybe to the Bradford club, at present City is the top dog and Bradford the bottom dog. Unless that fact is fully recognised it is useless to talk of amalgamation'. One correspondent even signed his letter 'Yorkshire Valley Parade forever'.

The following day, City's chairman Col. Armitage acknowledged the 'feeling of animosity of some of the old Manningham members towards any amalgamation with Bradford'. He did promise, however, that the committee would remain 'open minded' when receiving any proposal from Bradford. The members of the once-mighty Bradford club felt humbled by its fall from grace. The Bradford Daily Argus' Bradford RFC correspondent berated the committee, saying *they are courting indignity, and even ignominy, by an amalgamation proposal which can never be carried, and they are prepared to bow so lowly as to let Park Avenue to Bradford City with not a shred of Bradford pride remaining.*

Bradford City's three month lease on Valley Parade was one of the main topics of the amalgamation debate. Their landlord, the Midland Railway, was thought to be now more likely to give Bradford City a long lease, on the grounds that if Bradford City left Valley Parade, considerable traffic would be transferred to their railway rivals the Great Northern, whose Horton Park station served the Park Avenue ground.

The Bradford City committee was faced with three alternatives.

1. Obtain a long lease at Valley Parade
2. Amalgamate with Park Avenue
3. Develop a new ground

Two and a half weeks of debate had raged in the press and in the community when, at last, on 6th May 1907, the Bradford RFC committee decided to definitely adopt football, even if the amalgamation scheme failed. Harry Briggs said there was no time for the membership to be consulted, as the deadline for applications for Football League membership was 17th May. Meanwhile, after much lobbying from 'prominent citizens', the Midland Railway said it was impossible for them to give a definite answer as to whether Valley Parade would be required for future railway developments. However, they did give an assurance that they would not disturb Bradford City for at least three years.

With Bradford RFC seemingly set on an application for Football League membership, the sudden reopening of negotiations on 10th May was greeted by scepticism. 'Talk of Bradford's favourable prospects of election to the Football League is obviously a bluff', wrote the press. The Bradford City directors decided that the latest proposals would be put before a meeting of City members on 27th May. The proposal was as follows: the new organisation would be called Bradford City, Cricket, Athletic and Football Club; the finance and property committee would authorise an expansion of Park Avenue, and the management of football would be left with the existing Bradford City committee until their term of office expired. Then, all members of the new club would be entitled to vote new officials onto the football committee. Valley Parade would be retained for three years, unless its disposal was approved by the football committee.

Harry Briggs gave an interview on 14th May, denying, when asked, that given his family connections with Park Avenue he was being blinded by sentiment:

I look at this as a business matter. Here we have one of the best grounds in the country, a ground well adapted and reputed for other sports as well as football. The City team is one which should go forward into the first division, and they will need such a ground and such means of extension as there are at Park Avenue. We have offered to sacrifice the name of Bradford and have agreed that the club at Park Avenue be called Bradford City. It is a great task to win over the section of the club which keeps alive the old Manningham sentiment, but I have faith in this amalgamation. If there were two clubs in the city, one or other would inevitably take the lead, and it would be bad for the other. It would not be good for either. I may say this, and this is no threat, that once Bradford enter upon such a project as this we do not go back. If amalgamation should fail we shall go on. Our chance of getting a place in the second division is distinctly good.

Meanwhile, the former Manningham RFC captain Billy Fawcett urged Bradford City members not to be cowed by the choices facing them: *We are today in a better position than we have ever been since the ground was first made in 1886. We have struggled through years of hard work and anxiety, and now when we are better than ever before, we are asked to join the very club who could never scarcely 'thoil' us our very existence. They even threaten us with saying that they can easily buy themselves in the second division. Can they? They have always had a big opinion of their importance.*

A 'Valley Parade Defence Committee' organised a series of public meetings across the city. Ike Newton, a former Manningham player, proclaimed to loud cheers, 'it was not amalgamation, but confiscation'. Although an influential element of Bradford City members lived in Manningham, the club had attracted supporters from all over the city and beyond since the conversion to football, so members' letters in the press were by no means all pro Valley Parade, as here:

It was high time City directors and the so-called Manningham sentimentalists took up a more statesman like attitude and looked at it from the standpoint of what is the policy to adopt to secure the ultimate advantage and success of the club, for its present and future members and the association game in the city generally. Let the directors go in for the strong policy of unity and don't be over-influenced by the so-called Manningham sentiment. Which to people outside the Manningham area is beginning to be looked upon more as an object of pity than admiration. Should not the club have been named Manningham City and not Bradford City?

The popular mood was expressed in a letter in which a 'Valleyite' hoped that 'the City members will vote against the Valley Grabbers'. The Valley Parade Defence Committee met again at

Otley Road School. To loud applause the chairman of the committee said 'it has to be borne in mind that the Park Avenue committee is an autocratic body which has proved that it has the power to do what it likes, irrespective of a decision of the members of the club'. The final Valley Parade Defence Committee meeting was held at Drummond Road School. The six hundred members present were reminded that the school stood on the site of their former Carlisle Road ground, where the likes of 'Pongo' Richmond and J.J. Hawcridge had built the reputation of the Manningham club.

The evening of the 27th May 1907 saw the culmination of the amalgamation saga. Around fifteen hundred Bradford City members packed Westgate Hall to vote on the proposal. With emotions running high it was a brave man who stood up to speak in favour of the amalgamation. Thomas Paton did just that and, despite constant interruptions, he told the members 'if they rejected the scheme of amalgamation, that responsibility would be permanently be with them.' The former Manningham RFC favourite, Rob Pocock, jumped onto a chair and tried to address the meeting, whereupon the chairman, Col. Armitage said to laughter, 'I'm afraid you are offside again Rob'. The vote was taken, and a large majority (1,031 to 487) rejected the amalgamation. Bradford City would remain at Valley Parade.

Ultimately, it was the strong identity of the old Manningham club that had killed the amalgamation scheme. The reminders of continuity and use of rugby history to oppose the merger illustrates the forces that underpinned the opposition. Localised loyalties were decisive in preventing Bradford enjoying greater success in football where the competition was national and between towns and cities, rather than between districts. A merged club would arguably have been a formidable combination and could have established Bradford as a major football power.

The consequence of the vote was a split of support and resources that was to have a significant impact on the performance of both clubs. Harry Briggs's conclusion that two clubs in one city would do neither any good was ultimately proven correct.

Briggs had decreed he would press on with a separate football club in the event of a rejection of the amalgamation, and that is exactly what he did. Thus on 31st May 1907, Bradford (Park Avenue) AFC applied for membership of the Football League.

KICK-OFF

13
The Curious Case of Bradford (Park Avenue) AFC and the Southern Football League

A final piece in Bradford's sporting jigsaw was the bizarre occurrence of Bradford (Park Avenue) playing in the Southern Football League. Of course, it was a stepping stone to the club's ultimate goal of a place in the Football League. However, it brought about a deliciously contentious head-to-head between Bradford's sporting politics and those of the nation's capital city, at a time when the emerging dominance of London sport was being eyed with consternation by the industrial north.

Bradford (Park Avenue) faced powerful opposition in their bid for Football League membership, in particular from Southern League Fulham. Bradford's representative, the Reverend Leighton, told the Football League that the election of a second Bradford club would herald the 'extinction of Northern Union'. He endeavoured to talk up the club's civic status, saying that the lord mayor was the club's life-president; that three former mayors were vice-presidents, and four justices of the peace and two councillors were active members, and concluding that 'the Bradford club had the very highest and noblest of traditions'.

The Athletic News, reporting his speech, was snide. *This was evidently intended to impress the league with the majesty of the Bradford convert. Thus spoke the rev. gentleman who once referred to the Association game as "ping pong" and to professional players as "aliens". Evidently his conversion has been complete.*

Fulham's appeal was successful: they were elected to the Football League. To general astonishment, Bradford (Park Avenue) then applied for a place in the Southern League. Oldham Athletic, Bradford (Park Avenue), Southend United and Croydon Common vied for Southern League membership. Bradford (Park Avenue) promised £20 expenses to visiting London clubs, and £25 to clubs such as Plymouth Argyle travelling from further afield. Additionally they would pay two years' expenses on the first visit, and would bind themselves to the Southern League for three years.

Bradford's bid received an overwhelming twenty-six votes, while the champions of the Southern League's second division, Southend United, didn't receive a single vote. The Morning Leader newspaper saw Bradford's election as a historic step and one that would herald a mass migration of former Northern Union clubs into the arms of the Southern League, thereby transforming it into a national competition.

Others, notably two London papers, were less generous. The Daily Chronicle thought that the Southern League had overreached itself and, by ignoring its own second division champions in favour of Bradford's hard cash, had damaged its reputation, while the Daily Express wrote, *as both Bradford (Park Avenue) and Oldham have unsuccessfully attempted to gain admission to Division II of the English League, it looks as though the Southern League is content to play the role of a preparatory school for the elder boy.*

On the field, Bradford's Southern League sojourn was summed up as a 'brilliant beginning, a remarkable sequence of drawn games, nine consecutive defeats, and some steady improvement towards the close'. They were to finish a modest thirteenth. In early 1908, Tottenham Hotspur and Queen's Park Rangers announced that they would be applying for Football League membership. Two weeks later Bradford (Park Avenue) applied for Football League membership.

The Southern League's response to the crisis was uncompromising. At a special general meeting Bradford (Park Avenue), QPR and Spurs were told to resign by the 30th April. This was designed to place the clubs in a near impossible situation. It dared them resign from the Southern League without any certainty that their applications to the Football League would be accepted. A week short of the deadline Bradford (Park Avenue) resigned, a bold stance that they hoped would send a strong signal to the Football League.

Viewing the situation from the present, it is tempting to assume that the Bradford club had the weakest case of the three applicants. However, they were backed by the enormous wealth of Harry Briggs, plus the club believed they enjoyed a high status in sporting circles; in fact the Bradford Daily Argus described them as the civic team of Bradford: *Bradford have at Park Avenue an institution which ranked with Blackheath, Newport, Fettes Loretto and the best of rugby of all time [...] such an organisation must inevitably add to the importance of the league [...] the Bradford club is the town's club of Bradford, dedicated absolutely to sport and the public [...] almost a municipal club.*

Whether this made an impression in the boardrooms of the Football League is impossible to know. Citing matches against Fettes Loretto as proof of Bradford's importance might have been irrelevant; however, the club's past status as an elite rugby club clearly continued to be a central plank of the club's self-image. In some respects this has echoes of Bradford City members' use of Manningham's rugby history to illustrate their sense of identity during the failed merger bid. Clearly both clubs believed they had an organisational history and identity that overarched three changes of football codes. In choosing Bradford as the best illustrator of spectator sport's historic root and core, these curiously organisationally-rooted foundations of clubs' identities is something that sets the city apart from many others. Bonds forged even by previous generations - the value given to the group's sense of being an age-old establishment – seem to go deeper even than the commitment to the sport being played.

It would be a mistake to assume the Football League clubs were judging the candidates for league membership on purely footballing merits. Spurs, as FA Cup winners (1901), were the one side with a real pedigree, whilst Bradford (Park Avenue) and QPR were merely super-rich. The Bradford press thought Spurs was complacently resting on its laurels, relying on its name alone to get into the Football League. If true, then that was a dangerous game.

Bradford (Park Avenue) meanwhile was working hard to secure votes. The appointment of Gilbert Gillies, formerly of Leeds City, as manager of Bradford (Park Avenue) was highly significant, as it was commonly held that 'no man knows more about the politics of Socker football'. QPR's chances were fatally undermined when complaints were made about inducements being offered in the shape of travelling expenses. Of course, it was exactly the same policy that had gained Bradford (Park Avenue) a place in the Southern League, but attempting to buy off Football League clubs caused uproar, and QPR withdrew their application for Football League membership.

The annual general meetings of the Southern League and the Football League fell on the same day, 27 May 1908, and were held at exactly the same hour. Despite the months of jockeying for position, it was a close-run thing. Bradford (Park Avenue) edged out existing league club Lincoln City and at last successfully gained a place in the Football League. As the Bradford Daily Argus noted, *for the Bradford Association Club to gain admittance to the Football League a season after its formation has taken the football world outside Bradford by storm, and the force of that shock has been felt nowhere more intensely than in London, where a club like Tottenham Hotspur has been beaten.*

To modern eyes, the election of Bradford (Park Avenue) in preference to Spurs might seem illogical. However, there was a strong anti-metropolitan element within the Football League and in society as a whole. As the industrial might of the north declined, and society centralised, power and influence began to move inexorably towards the capital. Industrial provincial clubs still dominated the Football League; it was understandable that they were reluctant to loosen their grip. When viewed in that light, Bradford's bold decision to resign from the Southern League and then their patient but determined lobbying, in contrast to Spurs's complacency, may well have struck a chord in the Football League's boardrooms. Harry Briggs taking the club into the Southern League had demonstrated the seriousness and commitment of Bradford (Park Avenue) to professional football.

Bradford (Park Avenue)'s financial losses in the Southern League amounted to £1,360, although subsequent Football League membership reduced losses to £500. The extensive redevelopment of the Park Avenue football ground had seen the mortgage rise to £19,000. To fund the development of the ground, in 1909 seven thousand shares were offered, and the football club adopted limited company status. The Briggs family purchased 84% of the shares - a vivid illustration of the almost complete reliance of the infant football club on the largesse of this one family.

The formation of Bradford (Park Avenue) Association Football Club left the city of Bradford without a professional Northern Union team. As has been seen, supporters of the oval ball game had already begun to lay the foundations for a new Northern Union club. Though lacking wealthy benefactors, the proposed club could rely on the support of the Northern Union itself - which proved to be crucial as the game struggled to reestablish itself in Bradford. The game's governing body agreed to not permit the transfer of former Bradford Rugby Football Club players, and guaranteed a new club a place in the Northern Union. A bid to share Park Avenue was refused, and even an appeal for the redundant rugby stock was rejected. An entirely new club had to be formed. In time it would become known as Bradford Northern.

By June 1907 the new club had found a home at Greenfield trotting and athletics ground at Dudley Hill. Despite complaints that Greenfield was not on a direct tram route from the city centre, the average attendance for the 1907-8 season was around the four thousand three hundred mark. When compared to the previous season's average of five thousand at Park Avenue, the support levels appear to have held up well despite the move. Having said that, in the same season Bradford City's average league attendance was over fifteen thousand, and Bradford (Park Avenue) AFC's was going on for ten thousand.

In an attempt to attract more spectators, Bradford Northern moved to Birch Lane, an area that was described as being much 'more populous', was a short tram or train ride from the city centre and was less than a mile and a half from the club's former Park Avenue home. However, the facilities at Birch Lane were so poor that it was thought supporters of the Northern Union game preferred to travel to neighbouring towns to witness games. Bradford Northern would have probably not survived, had it not been for Bradford Council's development of Odsal Stadium in 1934 which finally allowed the club to escape from the constricting surroundings of Birch Lane.

Though the new Northern Union club was to face many years of struggle before it established itself, over a century later it is still active as the Bradford Bulls Rugby League Club.

14
A common goal

To recap on the start of this tale, the Industrial Revolution entailed an almost unprecedented movement of people into the urban environment. The parallel regularisation of working hours led to the creation of new living conditions and social interactions. With the eventual awarding of free time to the workers, a new concept evolved: 'leisure'. The evolution of 'leisure' was shaped by several factors: the exposure of the working masses to rapid urbanisation, an emerging civic culture, and elements of competition, commercialism and professionalism that were, and are, the bedrock of industrial capitalism.

This is the story of a revolution *within* a revolution – that is, the revolution of sport in the context of Britain's wider societal changes due to the Industrial Revolution. Bradford was one of what has been termed the 'shock cities' of the Industrial Revolution. Its sporting revolution was shorter and sharper than the industrial one within which it unfolded. In just half a century, Bradford's sporting passions were completely transformed from the informal and irregular to the structured and highly professional.

In many respects Bradford demonstrates in microcosm nationwide developments, and for this reason was chosen as the locus of this book. Much of what took place in Bradford had parallels in other towns and cities, especially in the north of England. It is nonetheless astonishing that, following a period of rapid and deep-rooted change, the sporting landscape that emerged in Bradford, of two professional football clubs, a professional rugby league club and a semi-professional cricket league, has remained more or less intact for a century.

The sports spectatorship that burgeoned and grew in Bradford and other Victorian cities has become a global phenomenon. There is little doubt that watching sport, and becoming a supporter of a (usually) local club, is a significant part of many people's identities in locations across the globe. Being a spectator has clearly always meant, and continues to mean, a great deal to a large proportion of those present at sporting events, wherever in the world they take place. Detractors of spectator sport who cite the sedentary and the commercial aspects of spectatorship fail to recognise this meaningfulness. Whether the experience of spectatorship has a spiritual dimension is another question: therein lies a whole other area of research.

But what has been particularly and uniquely compelling in Bradford's story is the phenomenon of the historical shift from Rugby Union to Northern Union, and finally to Association Football, of its two major clubs. The fact that the supporters of both clubs evidently put *organisational* loyalty before their loyalty to a particular sport speaks volumes about the linkage made by Bradfordians between sport and their sense of identity and belonging and pride, in what was effectively a brand new city.

That powerful sense of belonging has survived de-industrialisation and large-scale demographic changes. The fact that Bradford City has a Bangla Bantams supporters group, made up of first and second generation Bangladeshi migrants, is one demonstration of a Bradfordian sporting identity.

Thus in an age of globalisation, an identity that was initially formed around a suburban Victorian rugby club now serves this multicultural city's folk as a vehicle for cohesion and community, just as it did in the new industrial conurbation that was 1880s Bradford.

The wheel has come full circle.

Recommended books

The following list is intended as a guide to the interested reader looking for further reading related to the subject of this book. A list of all books, articles and other sources referred to in the original research is available with the PhD thesis which can be accessed via the link on the previous page.

Rugby and football

Burdsey, Daniel, *British Asians and Football: Culture, Identity, Exclusion* (Routledge 2008)

Collins, Tony, *Rugby's Great Split: class culture and the origins of Rugby League Football* (Frank Cass 1998)

Taylor, Matthew, *The Association Game, a history of British football* (Pearson Education, 2008)

Vamplew, Wray, *Pay up and Play the Game* (Cambridge University Press, 1988)

Vasili, Phil, *The First Black Footballer, Arthur Wharton, 1865-1930: An Absence of Memory* (Frank Cass 1998)

Walvin, James, *The People's Game, the history of football revisited* (Mainstream 1994)

Williams, Graham, *The Code War* (Yore Publications 1994)

Cricket

Birley, Derek, *A Social History of English Cricket* (Arum 1999)

Thompson, Arthur, *Odd Men In: a gallery of cricket eccentrics* (Museum Press Ltd, UK, 1958)

Social and sporting history

Various contributors, *Destination Bradford: A Century of Immigration* (Bradford Heritage Recording Unit 1987)

Hardman, Malcolm, *Ruskin and Bradford: an experiment in Victorian cultural history* (Manchester University Press 1986)

Holt, Richard, *Sport and the British, a modern history* (Clarendon 1989)

Hunt, Tristram, *Building Jerusalem, the rise and fall of the Victorian city* (Weidenfeld & Nicolson 2004)

Jennings, Paul, *The Public House in Bradford 1770-1970* (Keele University Press 1995)

Russell, Dave, *Looking North, Northern England and the national imagination* (Manchester University Press 2004)

Wright D.G. & Jowett J.A., eds., *Victorian Bradford* (Bradford Metropolitan Council 1982)

Women and sport

Williams Jean, *A Game for Rough Girls? A history of women's football in Britain* (Routledge 2003)

Velija, Philippa, *Women's Cricket and Global Processes: The Emergence and Development of Women's Cricket as a Global Game* (Palgrave Macmillan 2015)

Duncan, Isabelle, *Skirting The Boundary: A History of Women's Cricket* (Robson Press 2013)

Tate, Tim, *Girls with Balls: the secret history of women's football* (John Blake 2013)

McCrone Kathleen E., *Playing the Game: Sports and the Physical Emancipation of English Women, 1870-1914* (University of Kentucky Press 1988)

Owen, Wendy, *Kicking Against Tradition: A Career in Women's Football* (The History Press 2005)

www.ingramcontent.com/pod-product-compliance
Lightning Source LLC
Chambersburg PA
CBHW071350080526
44587CB00017B/3046